Sailed a Pretty Good Course

A son's discovery of his father's remarkable life story

Keith Neuman

Dedication

First, this book is dedicated to my mother, Joy Neuman, who helped teach me at an early age how to write. Very few come to benefit from a parent with a professional career in manuscript editing, and who cared that her children learned the proper skills.

And to my father, Jack Neuman, who I could not learn to fully embrace until it was much too late to do so in person. His inspiring life story would not end up being his to tell, but I think he would have been very happy to know I've taken on this task in the end. Perhaps in silently stockpiling his life story in photos and documents, he envisioned just such a project.

And especially to my beloved sons Alex and Nic; who I am grateful to say know their father well enough so that they will never have to contemplate writing such a memoir as this.

Contents

Preface vii

1: Introduction 1

2: Historical Context – Czech Jews and Family Roots 4

3: Early Years 17

4: Occupation and Escape to the New World 28

5: Becoming American 43

6: Back to Europe as a Ritchie Boy 63

7: Starting Life Anew – Once Again 96

8: A World of Travel 116

9: Family Man 134

10: Final Years 150

Acknowledgements 161

Sources 163

Endnotes 165

About the Author 173

Preface

This is the story of my father John (Hanus) Neumann – known to almost everyone as Jack Neuman – as told from my perspective as his son. I lost him when I was only 22, when I barely knew him as an individual apart from simply being my father. During our time together, we had a tense relationship that I think neither of us quite knew what to do with. His unexpected and sudden death at age 54 transformed my relationship with him in a profound way. As the years have gone by, I've learned about who he was and came to appreciate him as an individual rather than as a parent. Now, approaching 50 years after his death, it's time for me to tell my father's life story in written form in as much detail as can be assembled with the materials available.

What's the inspiration for this project?

First, I have embraced his story in my mind and my heart for many years; it has become an important part of my identity. But most of it wasn't written down or documented so that others – my family in particular – might know and appreciate this person, whom many have never met and might otherwise never know in any sense of the word. My immediate family has heard me regale some of the most noteworthy events in Jack Neuman's life, but oral history can be elusive. The only way to ensure his story doesn't disappear is to write it down.

My father's story matters in part because he was my father. But as much as this, his life was remarkable in its own right, and relevant to the time and circumstances in which he lived. In a nutshell: My dad came of age in the Sudetenland area of Czechoslovakia under the shadow of Nazi imperialism and anti-Semitism. Through persistence, resourcefulness and blind luck, he gained his freedom and his life as an 18-year-old refugee; returned to Europe to play a small, but strategic, part in ending World War II; then created a new life for himself in his adopted country as a trailblazer in the emerging foreign travel industry. And he had a family.

My father's story is part of a larger one that has formed its own literary genre. I have been inspired by similar stories about departed parents of Czech origin, two in particular. First, Helen Epstein's 1997 memoir about her mother (*Where She Came From: A Daughter's Search for Her Mother's History*), which relates a "quest for personal and historic understanding" that extends into the history of Jews in the Czech lands. And more recently, Ariana Neumann's 2020 memoir about her father (*When Time Stopped: A Memoir of*

My Father's War and What Remains); an account of a father who shared my own father's name and background, as well as another remarkable story of survival and finding a new life. These works present compelling stories that share a common historical and personal journey, and have provided me with a broad template from which to work.

This memoir is intended as a gift to important people in my life, notably my family and especially my children (and their children). Whether or not they come to appreciate its value remains to be seen, but such documentation will ensure that this family history doesn't disappear over time. It's also my hope that this effort brings my father and his story to life for my extended family members who knew him; they knew parts of the story – and, through this work, they'll come to know him better.

During my time with my father, he spoke little about his past life. But he kept an extensive treasure trove of family documents and photos dating back to his early childhood, which inexplicably he, and then my mother, held onto for many decades until they ended up with me. This includes a revealing 11 page autobiographical statement he was assigned to write by a therapist shortly before the end of his life, which I only discovered some years later. It is this material that makes his story possible to tell.

Ottawa, Ontario, Canada
April 2023

1

Introduction

We all have a father. The "who" and the "how" and the "relationship" are all infinite in variety, although certain patterns occur in families (such as "accepting," "adoring," "attentive," "absent," "abusive" and "aloof" – just to mention a few descriptors beginning with the letter "a").

For me, my father has always had a presence in my life, if not being especially "present." I'm now in my late 60s and he died suddenly almost 50 years ago, at age 54. So, for most of my life, he has existed in memories, photos and feelings. Even when my father was alive, his presence was limited because he was often not around, being occupied with his work, which sometimes included travel overseas. As the co-owner of a small, often struggling, travel agency, he seemed to focus his life first and foremost on his work; it's where he spent much of his time, and what I remember he talked about most at the dinner table. And when growing up, I didn't especially like being around my dad, and so didn't embrace opportunities to spend time with him.

So, I never really knew much about who my father was as a person. For me, as a child, he was somewhat of an embarrassment as a father; not like other American dads I saw on TV and in our neighbourhood. I was critical of him, and oppositional, as a child can be with a parent. It was never clear to me or to my parents why this was the case. In hindsight, I now think it was because we were very much alike in some ways, and this can often ignite sparks. And it may also be that I modelled some of my mother's behaviour; she was a judgmental person by nature and didn't go lightly on her husband. My opposition to my dad softened as I got older and gained more independence and maturity. But this also meant spending less time at home and with my parents, especially when I left for college at age 18. Less than four years later, he was suddenly gone, and the opportunity to get to know him vanished (not that this was a priority for me at the time).

But something remarkable happened at that moment when I lost him. In an inexplicable and powerful way, my whole conception and feeling about my father transformed, as if changing polarity from negative to positive. The opposition and criticism gave way to a strong feeling of closeness and identification. Over the subsequent years and decades, I have kept my father in my mind and heart; and from time to time when I think about him, feelings emerge that

I can best describe as a warm glow. As I have grown and myself become a father (also with two sons), I have come to appreciate him even more and sometimes try to imagine what his life might have been like. My father's life story is an important part of my own life story and identity. I feel proud of who he was, and can now appreciate how he was a remarkable role model.

It is a great story, but incomplete. So much is missing between the big moments and apocryphal anecdotes. My father never shared the full picture in his lifetime, and there remains some notable mystery. With 2021 marking the 100-year anniversary of Jack Neuman's birth, and the COVID-19 pandemic leaving extra time on my hands, it was the right time to dig into the extensive source material residing in the boxes of documents and photos that have been waiting patiently in my basement to be opened.

2

Historical Context – Czech Jews and Family Roots

Before launching into Jack Neuman's story, let's first set the context of where he came from; that is, his family background, the social context in which his early years took place, and its historical antecedents. How all of this shaped and influenced his life is impossible to tell, but we can know for certain that it did. For the purposes of this story, the history will not be comprehensive (as might be found in some biographies and memoirs), but will cover the high points that seem interesting and may be relevant to the tale that follows.

In this chapter, I lean heavily on the work of Helen Epstein's wonderful memoir of her mother and her mother's family, *Where She Came From: A Daughter's Search for her Mother's History* (published in 1997). Like me, Helen grew up in the USA as a child of a Czech Jew who survived WWII and the

Holocaust. While her primary focus is on uncovering family stories going back several generations, she also provides valuable facts and insights about the history of Jews in the Czech lands, which nicely accomplishes the heavy lifting for my purposes. I am indebted to her for this work, and acknowledge that I am drawing directly from her research and writing. Additional sources include what my father wrote about his family background in two short autobiographical pieces (described in greater detail later on).

Jews in the Czech lands

The term "Czech lands" refers to the regions of Bohemia and Moravia in central Europe, which make up the western and southern portions of what eventually became the country known as Czechoslovakia in 1918 (and which today is the Czech Republic).

Map of Czech lands (1928 – 1938).
(Society for the History of Czechoslovak Jews)

As Epstein tells it, the timing of the arrival of Jews in the Czech lands is unclear, but they likely came from Rome and Byzantium, and there are references to their settlement in Prague late in the 10th century. By her account, the initial period went smoothly in terms of relations with Christians until the end of the 12th century, when the Catholic Church began to restrict the freedom of Jews, as in other parts of Europe.

In this era, Jews were legitimized through charters as "serfs of the royal treasury," as subjects of monarchs who ostensibly provided for their protection. But these charters did not protect Jews from the Catholic Church, which condemned them as responsible for having killed Jesus Christ. As elsewhere in Europe, Jews in the Czech lands suffered under pogroms, forced conversions, and eventually the separation and expulsion from Christian society. Through the 13th and 14th centuries, Jews seeking safety from other parts of Europe settled in Bohemia and Moravia, which were comparatively less populated, and had fewer restrictions and more charters prohibiting forced conversions. Jewish families made lives for themselves largely (although not entirely) separate from Christians.

The Czech Jews survived the Middle Ages, often in the middle of the prolonged conflict between the German Catholics and the Czech Hussites (inspired by the Protestant Prague preacher Jan Hus, a Czech version of Martin Luther, who was burned at the stake in 1415). The Jews sometimes took refuge in Protestant areas, where they were less apt to be mistreated (as Protestants didn't view Jews as the anti-Christ).

Both Protestants and Jews found something in common from their persecution by the Catholics (who eventually defeated the Protestants in 1620). Throughout the 18th century, the Jewish population was severely restricted by imperial "Family Laws," which established a limit of 8,600 Jewish families in Bohemia and 5,400 in Moravia. This forced thousands of Jews to become illegal aliens, left to live in secret, and subsist on charity or leave for other countries. In smaller towns and villages, Jewish families might be fortunate to become leaseholders (called *Randars*) of land held by noblemen, which involved innkeeping, as well as the distillation and distribution of alcohol. These families often played a key role in small villages, as may have been the case with my predecessors.

The situation of Jews in the Czech lands changed dramatically in the late 18th century, when Hapsburg Emperor Joseph II (and his Empress Maria Theresia) moved to assimilate them into broader society. He eliminated the centuries-old laws that separated and excluded Jews, opened the door for them to pursue a university education, and allowed them to pursue work in areas previously forbidden to them. This opportunity for equality was unlike what Jews almost anywhere else could hope for, but there was a price to pay. Along with the new freedoms were requirements to "Germanize" in culture and language. The use of Hebrew was no longer allowed (official documents written in Hebrew became null and void), German language education was now expected (and required for those wishing to marry), and everyone was required to adopt a German surname.

While these changes were resisted in many parts of the empire, they were largely embraced in the Czech lands as welcome progress. They became the first large group of Jews in Europe to receive a secular education. As Epstein writes, "They embraced German culture as no other group within the empire."[1] Here lie the key antecedents explaining why Czech Jews became more secular than their counterparts elsewhere in Europe (including the absence of Hebrew and Yiddish that were the predominant languages used elsewhere in the Jewish world).

A half century later, the 1848 European revolution freed peasants from servitude and launched an unprecedented movement of peoples previously tied to specific lands. This was accompanied by the abolition of Jewish residence and family laws, prompting many Jews to leave the communities and neighbourhoods to which they'd been confined for centuries. These changes set the stage for my father's grandfather, Ignatz Neumann, to see his children spread out from the family homestead in Lasovice to make lives in nearby towns that were not previously open to Jews.

This newly won freedom of movement was not without its downside, as Jews moving into new areas were met with anti-Semitic resentment and resistance from both Germans and Czechs, often leading to looting and violence. Some Czechs resented Jews, perceiving them as agents of German industrialization. A significant event in 1893 was the Hilsner Trial, in which the death of a young Christian woman was blamed on a vagrant Jew named Leopold Hilsner. Like the more famous Dreyfuss Affair around the same time, the Hilsner case generated a clash between modern humanist thought and medieval superstition, and divided the Czechs. Hilsner was found guilty (likely on very flimsy evidence) and then convicted a second time upon appeal, and was ultimately saved from the death sentence by an imperial commutation to life imprisonment. According to Epstein, the Hilsner trial "was an enormous shock to Czech Jews," as it revealed in such stark terms their tenuous position within broader society. As Epstein further writes, responses to anti-Semitism varied, with some adopting a "corrosive self-hatred," while others became "proud militants."

Life for Czech Jews changed once again in 1918, with the end of World War I and the creation of the new country of Czechoslovakia. The country's' first President and spiritual leader was Thomas G. Masaryk, a progressive-minded and well-educated man whose intention was to base his new nation on the principles of American democracy (notably the Declaration of Independence), embracing the goals of pluralism, separation of church and state, freedom of the press, and even gender equality. He was brought up by a deeply-religious Catholic mother, and "imbibed anti-Semitism along with his mother's milk."[2] But, unlike other European leaders, he acknowledged his prejudices, and worked to limit the power and influence of the Church. Czech Jews were already largely assimilated, and encountered comparatively less hostility than did Jews in most other parts of the continent, where anti-Semitism was actively encouraged by the state.

Family farm building in Lasovice, 1975.

Family roots

Genealogical records available online indicate that my father's great-grandfather (Josef Neumann) was born in Mezno, and his son Ignatz was born in Poszdyne (both in the central region of Bohemia). But the story seems to begin in Lasovice, a very small village of 15 or so families near the Vltava River, between Prague and Plzeň (two of the largest cities in Bohemia). From what my father writes about the history, his predecessors rented the land from the Schwartzenberg family (whose ancestral home was the nearby castle of Orlik); and, following WWI, gained ownership of the land, which included a farm, a store, orchards and a small lake, as well as horses and cattle. The store was located in the middle of the village, directly across the village green from the large Gothic cathedral that served as the centre of the county. The region was almost entirely composed of ethnic (and Catholic) Czechs, and the Neumanns were one of only two Jewish families in Lasovice.[3] My great-great-grandfather (Josef Neumann) may well have been a Randar, as described in the previous section.

As my father writes in his brief memoir, on Sundays following church services, "the entire population of the district seemed to adjourn to my grandpa's store for a general discussion of the state of the world and it seemed only incidental that some commercial transactions also were carried out." That grandpa was the family patriarch Ignatz Neumann (although my father refers to him as "Hynek"), and both he and his father (Josef) were apparently well-liked and respected because they were generous with everyone (e.g., loaning money or cattle, offering advice). As Jack tells it, "This I know because I used to spend part of my summers there and all the people I met used to tell me what a wonderful man my grandfather was." (This eerily describes the way in which so many of my father's contemporaries describe their memories of him.)

Neumann clan in 1938 – my great uncles and aunts,
with teenage Hanus peeking out from the back

Ignatz and his wife Hermine (nee Engel) had a large family, as was common for established Jewish families in this time period – five sons and three daughters. There is a surviving family portrait that includes most of them as adults, taken around 1938 and subsequently annotated by another cousin. The photo depicts 12 people, including seven of the siblings, several spouses and, almost floating in the background, my teenage father (he looks as if he could have been photo-shopped into the picture). The eighth sibling, Josef, is missing, ostensibly because he had already moved away (it is his daughter Gertrude who later annotated the photo with the names and a few historical notes). Apart from putting faces to names, the photo is haunting because everyone is smiling and looking prosperous. Just a few years later, my father would be the only one still alive.

Little is known about the lives of most of these brothers and sisters, and only one of them survived WWII and the Holocaust. Josef (the one missing from the family photo shown here) was working in Milan when the occupation took place, and spent most of the war interned with his family in a small village in southern Italy. Ignatz and Hermine's eldest son Emil inherited the farm and properties, while brother Sigmund (who my father calls "Uncle Munde") rented another farm nearby in Holeśice. My father writes that the other siblings went to school in Prague and Vienna, and started various careers.

My grandfather Adolf was born in 1892, the fourth child and third son in the line (my father incorrectly refers to him as the eldest). My father writes that his father left the farm to go to Prague and Vienna, and during WWI served in the cavalry of the Austro-Hungarian empire. After the war, he ended up in Plzeň, an industrial town of about 120,000 situated west of Prague and just east of the border delineating the Sudetenland (an area bordering Germany and containing a large German-speaking minority). Adolf went into partnership with his brother-in-law Otto Immergut (husband to sister Emma) to either establish or purchase a sizeable candy factory in town, which gave him and his family a prosperous life. Family notes indicate the factory was located at Vyikalky #4, inside the walls of the famous Pilsner Urquell brewery, but other documents indicate a different location in the city, so perhaps it was moved at some point.

Adolf Neumann

As a successful young businessman, Adolf married my grandmother Emma Bergmann from the village of Kovarov, about five kilometres south of Lasovice. The Bergmann family tree is much better documented than the Neumanns', mostly thanks to the diligent genealogical efforts of a couple of family members. There is a Jewish cemetery hidden in the forest outside Kovarov (which I discovered on a visit in 2003), which has been beautifully restored and contains a number of impressive headstones (some up to eight feet in height). Emma's predecessors can be traced back to Adam Bergmann of Zbenice, who took the family name Bergmann around 1787, when Czech Jews were required to adopt German names.

Young Emma Bergmann (upper right) and her family, 1908.

Emma was the daughter of Salomon Bergmann and Elizabeth Aschermann, and had three sisters (Olga, Rosa and Marta). There is a lovely domestic photograph taken of the family. Olga married a Katz and had three children, two of which survived the Holocaust and went on to have children of their own; this line of cousins thankfully continues. Salomon had two brothers and two sisters; and from these came families that emigrated to the USA and became my treasured extended family of Czech American cousins.

The candy factory was likely successful, making it possible for Adolf and Emma to live in a spacious apartment at Veleslavinova Ulice 26 in the centre of Plzeň. Just a few years after the war, they were ready to start a family, which included two boys (starting a three-generation trend of two-son Neumann children), Hanus in 1921 and then Josef in 1926.

Emma Neumann, relaxing
at the farm in Lasovice.

3

Early Years

My father's birth certificate, issued by the Czechoslovak Socialist Republic, documents his arrival on October 4, 1921, in the Bohemian town of Plzeň, under the name "Hans Neumann." This German name has its roots in the Germanization of Czech Jewry more than a century earlier, and in the fact that Plzeň bordered on the German-speaking area, which later became known as the Sudetenland. Apart from the role of this region in the coming occupation by Nazi Germany, it also featured prominently in my father's early years. As he describes it:

> Between the two World Wars the Czechoslovak government was very "civil rights" minded and in addition to the two school systems [Czech and German], we had two operas, two professional soccer teams, and just about two of everything, whether we needed it or not. And that is the place I called home.

Plzeň was one of the country's largest cities, about 90 kilometres west of the capital city of Prague. In the late 19th century, its proximity to Western Europe helped the city become a major centre of industry, most prominently in automobiles (Škoda), railways and, of course, beer. The famous Pilsner Urquell brewery was founded in 1842, but has roots dating back to 1375 (the brand "Pilsner Bier" was officially registered locally in 1859). Like most of the country, the city's population was primarily Catholic (and in earlier times, was a centre of resistance against the Protestant Hussites). In the 1920s and 30s, the city had about 2,000 Jewish inhabitants, and an impressive synagogue (the second biggest in Europe) situated prominently in the city centre, where it still stands today.

Postcard of 1930s Plzeň sent by my father in 1940.
(He indicates his school in the upper left)

Being on the border between Czech and German population and culture, Plzeň and the surrounding area became a zone of contention and conflict. As documented on Wikipedia, following Czech independence from Austria-Hungary in 1918, the German-speaking minority in the countryside near the city hoped to be reunited with Austria; they later allied themselves with the Nazi Party after its ascension in 1933, with aspirations of being annexed. When the infamous Munich Agreement of 1938 resulted in the creation of the Sudetenland, the Third Reich effectively moved its borders to the city outskirts. This placed my father's family and other local Jews in the crosshairs, despite being almost entirely assimilated into broader Czech society and fluent in German, as well as Czech. As my father writes:

> We spoke Czech at home, but my parents could also speak German and on occasion they did, and as most of the Jews in town spoke German I was sort of looked at with suspicion. And life in a border town is not simple.

This linguistic and cultural borderland reality featured into my father's sense of himself from the beginning, as revealed by the way he opens his memoir in describing the complexities of his name:

> I know who I am, doesn't everyone? But do I really know? [This] illustrates my problem number one, or my first problem, quite well. I was given the names of Hans and Hanus, one German and one Czech and I learned only recently that during the first census of the then almost brand new country of Czechoslovakia my father listed himself as neither Czech nor German, but a Jew.

My English teacher [in Plzeň] gave me the name Jack, the English equivalent of Hanus I was told, but when I appeared before a U.S. judge for my USA naturalization I was told there was no such name as Jack which was just a nickname. So I was told that my name was John and it only shows how confused I was that when the judge asked me whether I wanted to change my name I now realize that he wanted to give me a chance to change it to Newman. I asked that one "N" be dropped from my name of Neumann. That's just for starters.

Hanus Neumann as a young boy,
August 1924.

We know little about Hanus Neumann's early childhood years. He writes that, when he was a boy, he was "quite close" to his father, who he describes as a "very kind and considerate man" with whom he took long walks and who "talked to me at length about everything and everyone as if I were an adult."

He goes on to write that his father also joked with him in ways that were confusing to a young boy, in one case musing about whether his son was in fact a gypsy child who was switched one day with the real son who, as a baby, was left sunning on a windowsill. He notes he never really believed this story at the time, but wonders why he still remembers "such a silly joke," implying it may have had a lasting impact on his sense of himself. He finishes the story by writing that my mother "blames me not infrequently for the same kind of 'gypsy humor,'" and this also rings true to me as well, in remembering what I thought of as my father's odd sense of kidding humour.

Most of what my father writes about his childhood centres on his schooling and participation in sports. A personal history statement he completed in 1948 for some bureaucratic purpose documents that he attended the Pilsen Grammar School from 1927 to 1932, and the Real Gymnasium high school from 1932 to 1936 (and graduating from both). Those are the basic facts, but the experience appears to be complicated. He writes that, at age 10, he faced his "first real crisis" in flunking the entrance exam to the Czech high school and ended up in a German-speaking one, which he describes as a "traumatic experience to find myself going to school with my enemies" (so-called because of earlier rivalries on the soccer field).

Hanus and his younger brother Josef.
(undated photo)

Sports featured prominently in young Hanus's life. His father enrolled him in a Jewish sports club (Maccabi) at age eight or so. He didn't take to gymnastics, but gravitated to football (soccer in North American parlance), and this grew to become his true passion. He describes how at Maccabi:

> We played all comers and our arch rival became a German
> [club] called Aar, an Aryan organization of the first order.
> Thus a game was not only a game but for us kids a political
> and "ethnic" event of great importance and a knock down
> and drag out fight on and off the field.

But his love of soccer helped him adjust to life in a German high school, and he writes that he soon found out that "they were really not such bad kids and it was not too long before I was playing football with Aar against Maccabi, my friends became my enemies and vice versa." He writes further that, when Hitler came to power a few years later, it "made my new schoolmates and friends increasingly restless" and he "found himself often at the center of the conflict." I wonder how he made this all work, and how this experience might have prepared him for the challenges he was to face in a few years' time.

Football also became the basis for what he describes as a falling out with his father, who opposed his son playing the game, which he saw as too dangerous. Hanus was determined to play and he continued, despite being forbidden to do so, with the help of the "whole town," which "conspired to keep my father in the dark." The situation came to a head when he was offered the chance to play for the junior team of the local professional club, with the help of two uncles who served on the club's board of directors. This he had to reveal to his father, who maintained his opposition to playing because of the risks. In an attempt to find a solution, they agreed his father would come to watch him play in a professional match, which he writes as having "never made a bigger mistake."

The game was against an Italian team from Bologna, and "was the bloodiest soccer match I ever saw and I watched plenty of them." Players were injured on both sides (badly enough that they couldn't return to play) and spectators also joined the fray by "throwing bottles and worse." He writes "there were plenty of bloodied heads to make everything look nice in red technicolor for my father who sat there with his mouth open." As he needed his father's permission to join the junior team, "that dream was shattered and I went back to [what he describes as] 'black football'." He goes on to write that "walking now on gimpy knees and rubbery ankles I finally understood my father's concern then, but in the late 1930s I could not understand him at all."

What amazes me to this day is how my father never once ever mentioned to me or my brother Eric anything about his football playing youth, or expressed any interest whatsoever in the sport as a spectator or fan. How could he as a father have never introduced his own sons to the game that he so loved in his youth? I think about this when I remember the time I started high school and had to decide whether to join the soccer or football team (since my wiser older brother informed me that everyone had to pick a varsity sport in high school). I don't recall my father offering any advice or opinion about what sport to choose, and it seems ironic that he supported my decision to go with football, which was clearly the more dangerous path (and would, in fact, result in several significant injuries).

Hanus riding his treasured racing bike.

About his high school education, he writes that his grades were generally good ("usually all 'A's"), in part because his father was quite strict about grades and demanded to see his report cards (flunking the high school entrance exam appears to have been behind this). When his "deportment grades" began to slip, this was never noticed by his father since they appeared in a different section of the report card, and parents weren't notified of low grades. He doesn't offer a reason behind his deportment troubles, but it may well have been about being a Czech Jew in a German high school. He writes that, by age 15 (i.e., 1936), "the situation became too sticky and I transferred to a Czech business school," where he then took up playing soccer for Czech teams, "for any team which played against the German school or Aar, or any other German team." Records show he attended a local School of Business Administration from 1936 until 1939 (when he then emigrated before graduating).

Parental conflict over sport surfaced again over a bicycle. Hanus had a treasured racing bike, "another dangerous toy my father wanted to save me from, in spite of the fact that every kid in town – and many girls – had racing bikes." On this matter, he won the day when one of his uncles bought him a bicycle for his birthday. He writes "this caused a row between the two men [his father and uncle] while I innocently and happily joined the bicycling fraternity." But, as with football, his father's fears were realized in a way that was to prove significant a few years later. One summer while at his grandfather's farm, young Hanus is speeding down a steep unpaved country road "going about 50 kilometres per hour" when a front wheel spoke breaks and he pitches forward onto the road, severely damaging the right side of his face. His face would eventually heal from these wounds, but with permanent scaring that remained with him the rest of his life.[4] And would also play a decisive role in saving his life.

All bandaged up from his bike accident.

4

Occupation and Escape to the New World

Jack's life through his teen years were in some ways typical of most young men his age, focused on school and sports. But, for him, it was also fraught with the ethnic tensions simmering in his world, and presaged what was soon to come.

Throughout the 1930s, Nazi Germany was rapidly arming itself and looking for opportunities to expand its boundaries and influence in Europe – with the goal of creating "lebensraum" (living space). In March 1938, it annexed Austria (an ethnically German country that welcomed this move). Later that year, Germany struck an agreement with other European powers in what came to be called the Munich Agreement, in which Germany would annex the Sudetenland on the pretext of protecting the vulnerable ethnic German population (of about 3 million) in the region.

Anticipating such ambitions, Czechoslovakia established treaties with Great Britain, France and the Soviet Union, committing them to come to its defence in the event of attack. But, in fact, none of these countries were keen for a military confrontation with Hitler's Germany, and conceded annexation of Czech territory in the hopes of achieving "peace for our time," as British Prime Minister Neville Chamberlain infamously boasted once the agreement was signed. On October 1, Germany marched into the Sudetenland and absorbed it into Germany proper. The rest of Bohemia and Moravia followed suit a few months later, in March 1939.

With Plzeň on the edge of the Sudetenland, becoming part of Germany was not good news for the region's small Jewish population and the Neumann family. The exact chronology of events that followed has not been fully documented, but my father writes:

> My father was among the first to be jailed, he was one of the many hostages the Gestapo had taken. We belonged to what I would call the upper middle class, were fairly well off, owned a small factory and belonged to some local clubs. I believe he was taken because at the time he was the Treasurer of a social club and they took all the officials of various organizations.

It is curious to note that he makes no reference to his father being Jewish, which must have been relevant, if not central, to Adolf's quick incarceration. Perhaps he doesn't mention it because it was so obvious, or perhaps it was a matter of denying the obvious. This description of his father's experience came from a lengthy letter he wrote me to support a college paper I was assigned, to write about my family history. The absence of a Jewish dimension to his family story is consistent with what my brother and I were told as children when the question came up about our missing paternal grandparents: that they were killed by the Nazis "because they had money."

My father writes that, initially, his father's incarceration "was not too bad," as he was kept in a local jail close to home and they could smuggle in food to keep him fed. But later, the Gestapo put the prisoners to work doing hard labour, marching them through the town to the local quarry. It was during such a march when Jack's mother Emma witnessed her husband being led back to jail "all bedraggled, worn out, limping and hardly being able to keep up with the rest," and she suffered a heart attack and died on the spot. Suddenly, young Hanus Neumann, at age 17 – with his father in jail and his mother suddenly deceased – was head of the family. His first task was formidable: to get his father out of jail to attend the funeral. Initially stonewalled by the authorities, he writes that he was coached by other family members to bribe a Gestapo official, which did the trick. My father never said any more about how he accomplished this, and I can only imagine how intimidating it must have been. But he pulled it off, and this was only the first of several such challenges he overcame with persistence and charm.

Photo of Emma Neumann, from her Trauer Album, prepared following her sudden death in 1939.

Hanus's mother – Emma Neumannova as she was identified in her Czech identification papers – was part of the Bergmann family, with a family tree exceptionally well-documented by my cousin Dasha Bergmann (who traced the line to Adam of Zbenice, a village in Bohemia). My father said almost nothing about his mother, either in his written memoirs or in conversations that I recall as a child. So there's no way to know what kind of mother Emma was or what my father felt about her. How he erased her from his written and spoken memories is indeed a mystery, and this must have taken its toll on him. I am saddened for both of us.

Emma was 48 when she died suddenly on the street in Plzeň. I have in my possession her "Trauer Album" (Grief Album), a small bound book of about 100 pages that must have been a common reference tool for family members to use for the funeral and subsequent mourning.

Most of the album is standardized text outlining Jewish prayers (e.g., the Kaddish) and other material that is typical for Jewish custom. It also contains a recent portrait of Emma and the customized dates for remembering her Jewish "Jahrzeit," for every year covering the period from 1940 to 1987 (i.e., the year, month and day, as well as the day of the week). I have had this album for many decades, and only now does it strike me how surprising it is that my father kept such a document, or possibly recovered it much later (along with other family possessions on a return trip to Plzeň many years later – a story recalled by one of my elder cousins, but not otherwise verified).

Emma Neumann's funeral – held in Plzeň's main cemetery – proved to be a decisive moment in young Hanus's life. As the extended family gathered at the gravesite to pay their respects, a conversation took place in which one of Hanus's older cousins (possibly Marie Vodička) suggested to him that he might go to the USA on a student visa, and live with her sister in Chicago.

Emma's gravesite in the Plzeň cemetery, 2003.

Before this, my father had already dropped out of school to concentrate on finding a way out of occupied Europe, with no luck; he checked into emigrating to the U.S., but was told the quota for Czech immigrants was already filled for the next 12 years or more. But student visas fell into another category, as this was considered a temporary status, and students were classified as visitors who would again be leaving after their studies; student visas didn't count toward the quotas for immigration. My father writes that he was encouraged to pursue this opportunity by his father, who saw no way to save himself or his younger son Josef (nicknamed Pepik), who was then too young to qualify as a student.

K. W. Kempf

General-Passage-Agentur

180 West Washington Street

CHICAGO   ILLINOIS

AFFIDAVIT IN SUPPORT OF APPLICATION FOR VISA.

I, *Louis Fisher* (Name), residing at *Chicago, Ill* (Street Address), *2800 Archer Ave* (City) (State), being duly sworn, depose and say:

1. That I (was born) (was naturalized) (declared my intention of becoming) a citizen of the United States on *6th May 1911* (Date) at *Sup. Ct. Chicago* (Place) the number of the certificate being (if naturalized) *189778*.
2. That I have resided in the United States since *September 1900*
3. That alien(s) desire(s) to come to the United States because *to better himself* (State reason fully)
4. That the financial status of the alien(s) is/are __________ (State whether or not alien is dependent on you for support and if so, to what extent)
5. That alien(s) previously resided in the United States from __________ (Date) to __________ (Date) and departed because __________ and (did) or (did not) declare his her/their intention of becoming an American Citizen(s).
6. My present dependents consist of: *1 boy and wife*
7. My regular occupation or call is *meat market* and my average weekly earnings amount to $ *100*
8. I possess property to the value of:
   Real Estate $ *30.000* — Personal $ *5000* —
   I occupy a __________ room house/apartment.
9. That it is my intention and desire to have my relatives whose names appear below, at present residing at *PILSEN Ahola jowa at 6 36 Brodo — Limova* (Give complete address) come and remain with me in the United States until such time as they may become self-supporting.

NAME	Married or Single	DATE OF BIRTH	PLACE OF BIRTH	PROFESSION or CALLING	RELATIONSHIP OF DEPONENT
HANUŠ NEUMAN		16 24 4. 1921	PILSEN Brodo-Vesoli	student	nephew

To the best of my knowledge and belief the above mentioned aliens are in good health and physical condition and able to read the [illegible] language.

That I am and always have been a law-abiding resident and have not at any time been charged with or arrested for any crime or misdemeanor. That I do not belong to nor am I in anywise connected with any groups or organizations whose principles are contrary to organized governments, nor do my relatives mentioned herein, to the best of my knowledge and belief, belong to any such organization, nor have they ever been convicted of any crime.

That I do hereby promise, agree and guarantee that I will properly receive and take care of them and that I will at no time allow any of them to become public charges on the United States, or any community or municipality of the United States and I do further promise and agree that any who are under sixteen years of age will be sent to day school and that they will not be put to work unsuited to their age.

Subscribed and sworn to before me, a notary public, in and for the County of __________ State of __________ this __________ day of __________ 19____ A.D.

(Notary's Seal)

My Commission expires __________

Affidavit provided in support of Hanus'
student visa application.

My father's path to freedom out of occupation was set in motion by his mother's first cousin Elsie Fisher (nee Vodička), who emigrated to the USA in 1919 or 1920 to marry Louis Fisher, the widower of her recently deceased half-sister Minnie. Elsie was our "Auntie Fisher," who lived to age 98 and was the matriarch of the many Bergmann cousins in Chicago. I remember her as a lively and strong-willed woman, who was likely a challenging personality for many others, but always kind and loving to young children like myself.

Elsie and Louis were particularly keen to sponsor her nephew, Hanus (Gene) Justic, but he was only 14 at the time and too young to travel on his own. So, my father was invited to chaperone his younger cousin on the journey to America. "So," as my father writes, "it was at my mother's funeral that the plans were hatched, in early May 1939." Realizing this plan required a number of essential documents and permissions from both sides of the Atlantic. The first was the easiest. By early summer, my father received a letter from the YMCA College in Chicago confirming admission, arranged by his cousin Rose (Elsie's eldest daughter, who was on a path to what became a long and successful career in teaching). Also arriving around the same time were the required documents from the Fishers, including an affidavit confirming their sponsorship of the two Hanus boys.[5]

The next step involved obtaining a passport and exit visa from the German authorities, including the Gestapo, who "had the final say." My father writes that both the U.S. and German authorities found the idea of two Jewish Czech teenagers going to the U.S. on student visas to be "ridiculous." But the key turned out to be persistence; as he writes, "For one time in my life I really wanted something and went after it." He goes on to add:

This consisted mainly of pushing my way over and over again into the Plzeň Gestapo headquarters, and the infamous one at Prague." [the one run by Adolf Eichmann who was then in charge of Jewish transport in Prague]. I kept being thrown out, laughed at, sent back for more papers.

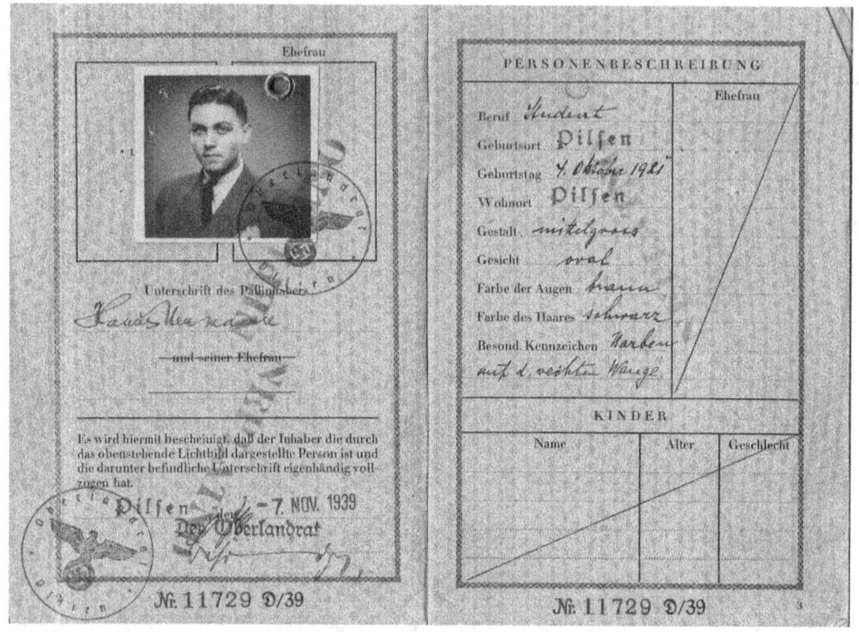

Hanus Neumann's exit visa, issued by the Gestapo
in early November 1939.

Hanus kept at this for several months, during which time World War II was now underway elsewhere in Europe, with Germany overrunning Poland and launching its Blitzkrieg into France. His persistence eventually paid off, helped in some measure by the injuries he suffered that summer from the bicycle accident on his grandfather's farm in Lasovice. He writes that, while they repeatedly turned him away, "they always treated me sort of gingerly – as if they had a guilty feeling, believing that one of their colleagues had worked me over in a very unprofessional way." He wries "the battered face brought me my freedom, or so I still believe."

Once he finally received his permission to leave occupied Czechoslovakia, the next stop was the U.S. Consulate in Prague, where he was told something was wrong with his papers and sent him back to the German authorities for "I don't know how many sessions." Once this shuttling concluded, he was informed by the Consulate that the regulations had since been changed and student visas were not longer being issued. But that didn't seem to stop him, and he caught yet another big break. He kept making a pest of himself until he was finally granted an audience with the Consul himself, who it turned out was also recovering from an injury. As my father writes, "his head was bandaged and his arm was in a sling. It must have been sympathy that made him give me a visa" (which, he later learned, the Consul was not in fact authorized to grant).

What did Hanus take with him on his journey to America (or, rather, what was he allowed to take)? Given the controls placed on emigrants, we have a detailed list among the many documents my father left behind. It is an official document signed and stamped at the Police Headquarters in Plzeň (dated November 27, just a few days before his departure).[6] The "undersigned office testifies that the things cited above in the register ... are the property of Hanus Neumann ... and will be transported from Pilsen to Chicago in America for the purpose of removal." The "things cited above" is a list (in Czech and English) of 65 personal types of items in what is listed as his "travelling trunk." Most of it was clothes and linen, including:

- 3 school suits
- 3 short trousers
- 1 featherbed
- 20 neckties
- 1 straw hat
- 1 table cloth and 12 napkins
- 1 bag with school necessities, books and dictionaries
- 1 pillow of gum

There were restrictions on taking newly-purchased goods, as the document verifies that "all quoted things are old and used, bought before 9/1/1938 [more than a year previous], with the exception of just a handful of items (1 suit, 3 shirts, 1 pair of shoes, 1 boat trunk, 1 sport shirt and 2 ties)." As was the case in Germany, the confirmed items were packed and the luggage sealed until placed on the departing ship.

Now with papers in hand, the two teenage cousins (Hanus and Hanus) had to find their way to a ship that would take them overseas. The only route at that time was through Italy, which was not yet at war. On December 2, they departed by train for Trieste, situated at the top of the Adriatic and the closest Italian port.

The MV Saturnia, which transported my father to the USA.
(Italian Liners Historical Society)

Arriving in Trieste the next day, they discovered their ship was not docking there and they would have to board it in Genoa, clear across the top of the Italian Peninsula (a journey of 550 kilometres). How they made it to Genoa in just a couple of days is not clear, and perhaps this part of the story was uneventful. Once they arrived and found their ship, the MV Saturnia, they were thwarted yet again. Somehow, their tickets were not in order and it looked as if they would not be allowed to board.[7]

Once again, fate favoured my father. This time, in the form of his Uncle Peppa (Josef Neumann, one of his father's brothers), who happened to be living near Genoa at the time. My father writes "I found him by a miracle, and with his knowledge of Italian and a lot of persuasion he got us aboard."[8]

The two cousins enjoying life at sea
enroute to America.

Finally at sea and heading to the USA, the journey continued to be an adventure. While on the open sea, the Saturnia was stopped by a French submarine, which ostensibly was removing all Czech citizens to serve in the Czech Army in Exile (then being formed in France). How did the two cousins avoid this potential disaster? As a boy myself, this is the part of his story I remember best. As my father once recounted, they hid in a lifeboat to avoid being found by the French resistance. Even then, fate almost delivered a knockout punch, when the departing submarine barely missed colliding with, and sinking, the ship.

This was such a thrilling story, and I always wondered if it was true. I once attempted to find out on a visit to Chicago in the 1980s when I invited his younger cousin (now called Gene Justic) to lunch so that I could ask him about their ocean journey to America. Nothing doing. He steadfastly refused to talk about any of it. As I came to learn later, Gene's unwillingness to revisit this part of his past persisted until shortly before his death, when he finally opened up (as told to me by his daughter Noel). Whether or not the lifeboat adventure did in fact happen as recounted, the fact remains the two cousins remained on the Saturnia for the remainder of their voyage to the New World.[9]

When the ship docked at Ellis Island in New York in late December 1939, the two young emigres were promptly "thrown in jail" on suspicion of being spies. Since the U.S. Consul in Prague was not authorized to issue student visas, their arrival was viewed with considerable suspicion. As my father tells the story:

> The immigration inspectors could not believe that we got student visas – they told us that all American representatives abroad were instructed not to issue any for fear that German spies might be using them – and we wound up ... in a special jail for anyone found inadmissible to enter the USA or for

people awaiting deportation. I got out right after Christmas, but then had to go to a U.S. Federal Court to get Gene out and I did that without a lawyer and not really knowing what I was doing.

His account is succinct, but how exactly did he pull this off? At just 18 years of age, arriving in a foreign country, with a limited knowledge of English and no one to help him, it's surprising how he glosses over this part of the story. Perhaps the many obstacles he was forced to hurdle over the previous six months in gaining his freedom from German-occupied Europe made this last one easy by comparison. His German-issued exit visa states he was accepted at New York, NY on December 27, 1939.

Once on American soil, my father quickly adopted the anglicized name "Jack" that was given to him by his English teacher back in Plzeň. I am told his young cousin was given the name "Gene" by his American cousin Florence Fisher.

Manifest from Ellis Island record of passengers arriving in NYC on December 21, 1939. (the entry for Hanus Neumann is highlighted)

5

Becoming American

As the 1940s began, young Jack Neumann was fresh off the boat in New York City, free of the Nazi occupation and ready to begin life anew in what Czech composer Antonin Dvork labelled "The New World." His knowledge of English had to have been limited, but sufficient to talk his way into the country, first at the Consulate in Prague, and then before a judge at Ellis Island. Because his young cousin Gene was not yet released into the country, Jack had time to kill in the city before proceeding to their sponsors in Chicago.

His memoir says almost nothing of his time in NYC, and his official personal history statement does not list an address there, but he made the most of his short time in the city before moving on to live with his cousins in Chicago. There is reference to two individuals in NYC with whom he likely stayed, George Hermann (whose mother lived in Plzeň, hence the connection) and Franz Seidler.[10] What did he do in the Big Apple?

Newly-arrived Jack taking in the view
from the top of Rockefeller Center.

What we have to go on are a few tantalizing photos and a brief letter he received from George Hermann some months later. One photo is taken of a smiling Jack Neumann atop the Rockefeller Center, with the Empire State Building rising out of the mist in the background.

The other two are taken in the famous Cotton Club (at the time housed in the Rockefeller Center); one is a standard celebrity photo of a performing Louis Armstrong, autographed with *"Best Wishes to Jackie Neumann from Louis Armstrong. ol Satchmo."*[11] The second photo (in a sleeved cover) is taken of my father sitting at a table with a young woman; she is smiling and looking at my dad, while he gazes intently at the camera. Above the photo it reads: *"To Jack, from Maybelle with love."* And below, once again from Ol Satchmo *"Best wishes from Louis Armstrong."* Opposite the photo on the inside cover, there is another autograph, *"Sincerely Maxine Sullivan"* (she was a well-known vocalist who performed with Louis Armstrong at the time). It must have been quite a thrill for the 18-year-old just arrived from western Bohemia.

Jack and his date at the Cotton Club,
with Louis Armstrong autograph.

The letter adds a bit more context about my father's brief time in NYC. It is one of several received from George Hermann – all but one are in Czech (and remain untranslated), but one is in English, as George acknowledges he was too busy to write this one himself, so dictated it to his secretary. The letter is dated February 3, 1940, after my father left for Chicago and had time to write George both a card (likely a thank you card) and a letter. George's letter covers a few topics, but most notably money and women. The former is described as the "Fried matter," in which a Mr. Fried is described as having failed to forward funds that George's parents (ostensibly in Plzeň) gave him for this purpose. George writes that Mr. Fried never wrote to explain why he never sent the money, and asks Jack to "call him up again and tell him I would like to have a direct explanation from him," and indicating that, if this does not arrive, he'll have to take serious steps. There are no further records revealing what ever happened on this issue.

George also mentions two women who they both may well have dated. He says he received a very nice letter from Brazilla, which referred to a "dinner appointment" she had with my father. He goes on to implore my father to write him about how he likes her and his "frank opinion." Later, he asks Jack that, if he sees Brazilla, to give her "my best love." George also recounts having recently gone skiing with Maybelle (of the Cotton Club photo, no doubt), and that they had a great time together.

My father must have written to George about challenges in his first job in Chicago, and George counsels him "not to be afraid" and that "beginnings are always rather hard." He goes on to offer to provide any advice or help, and that "I will do anything I can for you." Such a good friend.

Given the evidence, Jack clearly adapted quickly to life in big-city America. But it was not quite what he was used to at home. A story he later recounted involves one of his first encounters with the local cuisine. In one of those early days, he happened upon a hot dog stand and eagerly purchased his first American hot dog, expecting something like the tasty sausages he had enjoyed in his youth. He also ordered a root beer to wash it down, fully expecting it to be actual beer.[12] This proved to be a bitter disappointment, and likely not the last in his experiences in his adopted home.

Sometime later in January, Jack moved in with his sponsoring cousins at 2880 Archer Avenue on Chicago's West Side (today this site has been replaced by major Interstate highway I-355). This is listed as his address of residence until September 1941, when he left for college. Being on a student visa, Jack wasn't allowed to work, and his educational options were limited because he "had no money to go to school and besides colleges would not accept my credit" for his Czech education.

Jack (far left) and Gene (far right), with
their sponsors Elsie and Louis Fisher.

So, he had to proceed with the original plan of enrolling as a senior at the Central YMCA College Day High School, which had accepted him the previous year as part of his student visa application. He completed the year successfully, as documented in a diploma dated January 22, 1941 (which he kept and I now have in my possession). He was a good student, as attested in his report cards (also kept), which show mostly "A"s and "B"s in his studies (American History, Business English, Civics, General Sciences, American Literature and Typewriting).

Although my father wasn't eligible to work, he did so anyway on a part-time basis while completing his final year of high school. Jack started first as a clerk at the Bata Shoe Store – perhaps he was hired there because Bata was founded by a Czech. That job started in February 1940, and records show it lasted only a month, before he found a better opportunity at the Leader Department Store just down the block. He started as clerk, and was later promoted to assistant to the manager, and he continued working there until leaving for college more than a year later.

Acquiring a U.S. high school credential was an important milestone to future plans for education and career, but it also meant that his student visa would expire and he could be deported back to occupied Czechoslovakia. As he writes:

> Uncle Sam turned out to be made of sterner stuff than my father and I had to carry on a running battle with the Immigration Service against deportation back from where I came. Throughout my senior year at high school I was making application[s] to colleges – entrance and scholarship. Fortunately, I had found another Czech in similar circumstances, older and Oxford-trained, who helped me with all the unfamiliar forms, letters and interviews. Results after about 60 or more applications = absolutely nothing.

His German-issued exit visa was set to expire on May 6, 1940, and the U.S. one issued at the Consulate in Prague was good until September 5 of that year. Close to the deadline, on September 3, he managed to get an extension to May 6, 1941 (so extending his German visa to a full year). The hoops he had to clear to avoid deportation were further indicated by additional stamps in his visa from the German Consulate in Chicago, dated November 6,

1940 and July 6, 1941. Since the USA had not yet entered WWII, it maintained diplomatic relations with Germany and abided by the rules it imposed on people under its jurisdiction. My father had to negotiate a careful path between the two nations.

College fraternity class picture. (Jack is in the back row, second from the left)

It seemed the only way Jack could remain in the country was to enroll in college, and his prospects seemed to be disappearing. Then, "out of a clear blue sky" comes an offer from the president of a Jewish fraternity at the University of Wisconsin in Madison (Phi Epsilon Pi), covering enrollment and a full scholarship to cover tuition, room and board. Apparently (from my mother's own memoir), this fraternity created scholarships for Jewish students as a contribution to the war effort overseas, and somehow found my father (he writes he never learned how they did so, but was certain it wasn't from the many applications he submitted). In September 1941, just a month before turning 20, Jack Neumann was on the move once again, this time 150 miles north to attend college in bucolic Madison Wisconsin. It was there that he met my mother.

Joy Goldstein was the elder of two daughters in a secular middle class Jewish family in Chicago. Both of her parents arrived in the USA from eastern Europe as infants, and grew up in the burgeoning Jewish community on the city's West Side. Her father – Henry G. Goldstein (originally Hansel Havas) was a world-class athlete (most notably for speed skating, but also in track and field) – he qualified for the 1928 Olympics in pole vault but was unable to compete due to injury. He became an accountant at Isenberg and Sons, known for its costume jewelry.[18] Her mother, Lillian Goldstein (originally Pia Leah Friedman), was the daughter of a kosher butcher, and trained to become a stenographer (work she performed part-time until well into her senior years).

Joy Goldstein (undated photo)

My mother was a singular individual in many notable respects and deserves her own story (which she recounts through her own partially-completed autobiography). She demonstrated exceptional intelligence from an early age (e.g., skipping two and a half years in grade school), and was destined for more education than was typical for women in her age and social class. At just 17, Joy left home for the first time to start college at the University of Wisconsin in the fall of 1941.

How did Jack and Joy meet? My mother nicely answers the question:

It happened this way. I was coming back on the train from Christmas break in Chicago and of course the train was full of students returning to Madison. I was sitting with a boy I'd been dating a fairly short time – a real nerd. He belonged to a fraternity (Phi Epsilon Pi) and offered me a lift to the house when we got to Madison, as a fraternity brother was meeting him with a car. Very few students had cars at that time. Not surprisingly for the midwest, it was snowing. The fraternity brother turned out to be none other than Jack Neumann, whom I had not met before. He was trying to open the locked trunk of the car, unsuccessfully, to deposit our bags. For some reason, I offered to help with the lock— my manual dexterity then wasn't any better than that it is now—and to my everlasting astonishment I was able to open the trunk where he had failed. What a laugh.

That "broke the ice" in her words, and she was attracted to his good looks and "delightful foreign accent." After a bit of delay, they started dating on a regular basis. My mother recalls one "memorable afternoon" when my father rented a boat to take her sailing on Lake Mendota by the college campus. Predictably, the wind died in the afternoon and they failed to return in time for dinner at their respective houses. By the end of the college year, she writes, "I was very fond of him and of course imagined myself in love."

Jack and Joy in courtship.

When the Japanese bombed Pearl Harbor on December 7, 1941, the U.S. finally entered World War II. My father tried to enlist (no doubt, he was keen to join the fight in Europe), but wasn't accepted because he was considered an "enemy alien," despite coming from an occupied country (it seems unlikely the U.S. government treated expatriate French or Poles in the same way). He writes that the Czech Army in Exile wanted him, but "by then I did not want them — and while I was perfectly healthy their examining doctor found me unfit." So, he continued with his college studies (which he notes was "with honors") until he was eventually drafted into the U.S. Army a year later.

Jack didn't finish his second year at the University of Wisconsin but, as my mother writes, was given full credit for the year "because of his patriotism in joining the Army." He received a certificate from the University confirming the title of "Junior Graduate in Liberal Studies," based on satisfactory completion of two years of study in the College of Letters and Sciences (dated January 23, 1943). His official college transcript shows he earned "A"s and "B"s in all subjects taken, except for a "C" in a first-year basic science course.

Jack was officially enlisted as of February 1, 1943, and was shipped off to basic training for three months and then naturalized as a U.S. citizen (at the Circuit Court Winnebago County, in Rockford IL, on April 9, 1943). It was at this point that he chose to modify his last name by dropping the last "n," to become Jack Neuman. He never wrote or commented about why the name change (nor did my mother make any mention of this), but I imagine he felt the new spelling was more American and less apt to be misspelled (boy, was he wrong about that).

Following basic training, recruits were given the opportunity to list which branch of service they'd like to join and, according to my mother, Jack put down the Air Force (which was separate from the Army and apparently a popular choice). Instead, he ended up in the Medical Assistance Corps, which was quite a disappointment, since it wasn't front-line work that involved fighting the Nazis. Like other "enemy aliens" now drafted into noncombatant ranks, he was sent to Camp Barkeley in June 1943, the basic training center for medical administration located outside Abilene, Texas. As recounted by another soldier, training at Camp Barkeley included lengthy hikes under the hot sun carrying heavy field packs, along with classroom instruction by local high school teachers about the fundamentals of paperwork for medical treatment and hospitalization.[14]

Not surprisingly, Jack was keen to find an escape and did so by successfully applying for Officer Training School. In September, he became a Platoon Leader with the 119th Medical Corps, attached to the 44th Infantry Division at Fort Lewis, Washington, followed by a stint doing preparatory maneuvers in the swamps of Louisiana. This was not an improvement in his situation. But then his fortune changed again early the next year, as he writes:

> My 'god out of the machine' went to work again and I was plucked out and deposited in a military intelligence training camp [at Camp Ritchie MD] in the charming Blue Ridge mountains, and taught how to interrogate prisoners of war.

Somehow, the Army finally recognized his value in being fluent in German (and well-motivated to take the fight to the Nazis). In February, 1944, Jack begins his true military career at the foot of the Blue Ridge mountains in western Maryland.

Just a month or so later, when Jack was on leave in Chicago visiting Joy, he brought up the topic of marriage, which he did so obliquely (to my mother's irritation). She turned him down "vigorously" because she had clear ideas about how she wanted to do other things (like travel) before settling down to marriage at age 25. Yet, once he returned to training camp, she pondered what to do. As she writes:

> I still felt I was too young (at 19) to get married, but the other side of the equation was that, knowing myself, I'd find some other guy to fall in love with before Jack got home and thus I'd lose him. An important factor was that Jack knew he was being sent overseas in two months. Finally, I decided that Jack was too great a person to risk losing, and that I wasn't prepared to take that chance.

Following a frantic week of "heavy mail and phone traffic" (with her mother hand delivering to her workplace every incoming letter from Jack as they arrived), the offer of marriage was accepted. Her father then wrangled train reservations to get Joy and her parents to Hagerstown, MD, the town closest to the Army base at Camp Ritchie (18 miles away); this was not an easy thing to arrange, as trains were filled to capacity with servicemen coming and going. Off they went, this being Joy's first trip outside the Midwest, and she writes she found the train travel as exciting as the forthcoming marriage. She also had second thoughts:

> I suddenly realized, as we drove out [to the camp gate] that
> I didn't remember what he looked like, and experienced a
> sudden bout of terror as to what I was getting into. However,
> as soon as I saw him, all doubt dissolved.

Meanwhile, the young groom had his own challenges with organizing a wedding, and having to do so without his bride's input. In those days, most weddings were officiated by a religious authority, and my father found a local Orthodox rabbi (Jeshaia Schnitzer) to do the honours. It turned out to be this rabbi's first wedding ceremony, and neither of my parents had any experience or knowledge about Jewish marriage protocol. The ceremony took place on March 29, 1944 in a bare room occupied by the marriage couple, Joy's parents and four young men struggling to hold up the chuppah (wedding canopy), which teetered as the ceremony unfolded. When the time came for the groom to break the ceremonial glass (wrapped in a napkin) – symbolizing that, even on such a joyous occasion, all is not all right in the Jewish world – it took Jack several tries to finally succeed.

The newly-wed couple and Joy's parents then went back to the hotel to celebrate, and Jack then needed to affect a room change so the newlyweds didn't spend their wedding night adjacent to the in-laws. Once the parents went back to Chicago, Jack and Joy finally were alone together as man and wife, and made the most of it over the next two months – first in Harrisburg and then back in Hagerstown, which was closer to the camp – until he was sent overseas in late June.

On their honeymoon in Maryland.

In his memoir, my father looks back at that time in an unusually revealing way:

We had known each other about two years and during this time both of us let go and tried with other potential partners but came back. I believe that I was still a roughneck farmer and I must credit Joy with bringing out some tenderness and love. Looking back now I admit to myself that it was not only love and passion, but also a desire to be part of something more than myself – to have some family to come home to as I had not heard from my own family for some time and was really all alone. I had many friends then, friends to visit, to have fun with, to write to – but it didn't mean much. A friend was there one day, gone the next. Now I would think that marrying a tender young thing on the way to war was reckless, thoughtless and not a little selfish, but it seemed the right thing to do at the time.

Jack was indeed alone without a family of his own, having left his native country almost four years earlier. Throughout this time, he received numerous letters from his father Adolf, and in a few cases other family members. And this correspondence must have mattered a great deal because he kept these letters for the rest of his life, and they eventually came into my hands. The letters were written in Czech and sometimes German, both of which were inaccessible to me. In the 1990s, I became interested in these letters and managed to convince two of my older cousins to translate about a dozen of them into English. The translated letters date from late November 1939 to August 1940.

This correspondence covers what one might expect a loving father to write to a cherished son who has left home to make a new life in a distant land, and are very moving (even in translation). In the first letter, he laments the fact that he is unable to see Jack before his departure (he doesn't have his identification papers in order), and prays to God that he protects his son "always and everywhere."

In subsequent letters, Adolf continues to express both hopes and worries about his son's journey, admonishes him to never forget his family, and gives further advice on various matters ("never forget your dear saviours, Aunt and Uncle Fisher," "always without hesitation do what is asked of you," "never look to people of bad character," "never play with your health," "never make debts," "Always remember your dear mother who saved all her life."). In one letter, he adds a short note to the Fishers, thanking them for their sponsorship ("a great Jewish hearty mitzvah"), and asking them to be "patient with the boy" and to "be strict with him and he must listen and obey what you consider is proper and he must be thrifty and must accurately account for his finances."

The letters also provide news from home, mostly about family members. Several times, his father expresses worry about Jack's younger brother Josef, who was experiencing health issues and seemed to be socially withdrawn. Adolf writes about family members and Jack's contemporaries, some of whom are waiting to emigrate (including one couple soon departing for Palestine). In one letter, he "begs" his son to speak with his American cousins about how Jack's first cousin Karel might find a way to get to America ("tell [them] he is a grandson of Ignatz of Lasovice, as are you").

The letters don't say much about the occupation and treatment by the Nazis, but it's clear that conditions are deteriorating over the course of the few months covered in this correspondence. Adolf mentions taking in boarders, and later renting out their living room for income, with he and his son moving to the bedroom. In the early letters, he talks a bit about the family business, the candy factory RINA, which he runs with his brother-in-law; by February 1940, he writes about needing to find a buyer for the business, and by April he laments about having "a long day to fill with nothing to do" with his time.

In the same February letter, he writes to Jack about a new law that requires the payment of "an emigrant tax plus supplements" that must be paid when a family member leaves the country, a tax he says would amount to "the total inheritance from your dear, departed mother" (as written, but may well have included the total family wealth). Adolf believes they may be exempt because Jack left on a temporary student visa with the expectation of return, and begs his son to obtain the necessary notarized documents in the U.S. in duplicate and "<u>send one set immediately by the fastest airmail</u> and the other by regular registered mail in the event the airmail should be lost." There is no further information about what ever became of this and, in the end, it would not have mattered. The official Nazi records document that Adolf Neumann and his son Josef were put on a transport to the Terezin concentration camp on January 18, 1942.

6

Back to Europe as a Ritchie Boy

Camp Ritchie is located at the foot of the Blue Ridge mountains in western Maryland, not far from the Civil War battlefield at Gettysburg. In 1942, the U.S. Army turned Camp Ritchie into the Military Intelligence Training Center (MITC), a school to train recruits for work in intelligence and the interrogation of Prisoners of War (POWs). The location was ideal in terms of being close to Washington, and at the same time remote enough to discourage casual visitors and foreign spies.

What made Camp Ritchie unique was who got recruited for this specialized training. Once the USA entered WWII at the beginning of 1942, the Army realized it was sorely lacking the intelligence capabilities required for executing a war against Nazi Germany. Based on the British model, the decision was made to centralize the training for the Army's interrogators, interpreters and translators, and

Camp Ritchie was leased from the State of Maryland in June 1942 for this purpose.[15] An excellent description of the camp is provided by Bruce Henderson in his 2014 book, *Sons and Soldiers*:

> A camp theater was constructed for propaganda training sessions, which would one day include mock Nazi rallies with a Hitler look-alike... For instruction in conducting raids and house searches while avoiding enemy booby traps, an authentic-looking German village was built; its facades resembled the back of a Hollywood movie studio. This was done... with a level of security second only to that given to the development of the atomic bomb at the Manhattan Project, which started that same summer in Oak Ridge, Tennessee.[16]

Administration building at Camp Ritchie MITC.
(Maryland State Archives)

The Army also recognized that it could make excellent use of its soldiers with German backgrounds – native-born Americans from German families and expatriates who grew up in German-speaking countries. This latter group included a significant proportion of Jews, some of whom who fled the oncoming Holocaust as refugees. Most were by no means natural soldiers, and many were intellectuals and "misfits" (as described by one of them in a retrospective interview). But they had an excellent knowledge and understanding of the German language and culture, which meant they were uniquely equipped for intelligence work in the European theatre. The Ritchie Boys (as they became known) played a critical role in the Allies' victory, by one estimation accounting for 58 percent of the Army intelligence produced in that theatre of war. In all, roughly 20,000 men were trained at this location between 1942 and 1945.

The eight-week training program at Camp Ritchie was extensive and rigorous. Among the courses and skills included:

- Learning the "Order of Battle" covering the entire structure of the Germany army, which could prove useful in demonstrating to prisoners a superior knowledge of their units. All of this had to be memorized, as such written material couldn't be taken to the front;

- Terrain and aerial intelligence, including how to draw topographical maps, interpret aerial photography, and send and receive Morse code;

- Hand-to-hand combat techniques, including how to garrote a sentry from behind;

- Weapons training, covering various models of rifles and pistols; and

- Field training, involving running obstacle courses and crawling under simulated or live fire.

Interrogation training at Camp Ritchie, which took place with actors and sometimes captured German POWs.
(Maryland State Archives)

Most recruits were trained as Interrogators of Prisoners of War (IPWs), which was perhaps the most extensive part of the curriculum. They were instructed in how to use a variety of techniques designed to extract tactical information, which included four basic strategies:

- Demonstrating superior knowledge, in which prisoners were overwhelmed with details about enemy units so they might be enticed to divulge yet further information;

- Offering forms of bribery, such as eating a chocolate bar or lighting up a cigarette in front of prisoners, and offering similar to prisoners once they cooperated;

- Finding common interests, to play on a prisoner's own preferences and likes; and

- Using fear in ways that fed on a prisoner's anxieties and vulnerability, with the hanging threat that something terrible might happen if they did not cooperate.

The available evidence indicates that physical abuse was not part of the interrogation regimen. As recounted in Henderson's book:

> In case any of the students got the idea there were no legal or moral boundaries when it came to prisoner interrogation... the rules and regulations [state] 'First and foremost, and remember this if you recall nothing else... Never touch a prisoner. That is a clear violation of the General Convention on Warfare.'[17]

The Ritchie Boys's contribution went unacknowledged for many decades due to the U.S. government's reluctance to disclose anything about its intelligence operations. But eventually the story emerged, initially through an Academy Award-nominated documentary by German director Christian Bauer, *The Ritchie Boys*, released in 2004.[18] This feature-length documentary included in-depth interviews with half a dozen Ritchie Boys, along with revealing archival footage. The story has been further recounted through numerous books (both fiction and non-fiction), and a recent TV segment aired on the CBS television program 60 Minutes.[19]

Jack at training camp.

This was the perfect assignment for the young Jack Neuman, who arrived at Camp Ritchie as a Second Lieutenant in February 1944, itching to take the fight back to the Nazis who occupied his home country and terrorized his family.

My father wrote almost nothing about his military experience in WWII, and my mother devotes no more than a few paragraphs to that time in their lives. But, for some unknown (and unknowable) reason, my father preserved an extensive collection of documents and photographs covering his wartime service in the U.S. Army. This includes extensive Army correspondence and "orders" pertaining to his deployment and service record. From this and other correspondence, it's possible to reconstruct in some detail his postings, positions and activities while serving in Europe.

Jack Neuman's records indicate that he trained at Camp Ritchie from February to May 1944, graduating as part of Class 17 (German language and assigned as an IPW Officer, Assignment VI: 879). At the end of June, he sailed from Boston on the RMS Aquitania and arrived first in Scotland on July 8, 1944. He was attached to the U.S. 5th Armored Division, and landed in Normandy on July 24, 1944 (roughly six weeks after the D-Day landing at the same location). Ritchie Boys were organized into small groups of six that were attached to Army units, and operated with considerable independence in carrying out their duties.

RMS Aquitania, which took Jack back to Europe.
(U.S. Library of Congress)

Archival records identify the members of IPW Team 879, with my father – at just 22 years of age – one of two commanding officers (rank, name and serial number).[20]

- 2nd Lt Bronnek, Gary H. (01169039)
- 2nd Lt Neuman, John H. (02047762)
- M/Sgt Michaelis, Rudolf H (39007411)
- S/SGT Wolf, Harold H. (36727103)
- T/3 Bruno, Ernest H. (32806792)
- T/5 Mark, Walter M. (32300681)

Jack's Army dog tags.

The records show that Jack followed the 5th Armored Division through northern France and the Rhineland campaigns, as the Allied troops slowly pushed the retreating Germans back into their own country. In order to obtain intelligence that was as current as possible, the interrogations took place as soon as prisoners were secured, and typically at or near the front lines, along with the fighting troops. Needless to say, this added an element of danger and risk to the work, as recounted by Ritchie Boys in contemporary interviews.

Jack busy with intelligence work, likely somewhere in France.

Like some Jewish Ritchie Boys, Jack chose to have dog tags[21] that did not identify his religion. This was a precaution taken in the event of capture by German troops, who would likely be harsher in their treatment of Jewish prisoners of war.

My father never spoke much about his experience in the field, and this isn't covered in the official documents he kept. But through the stories and memoirs of other Ritchie Boys, it's possible to get a good idea of what it was like to carry out his responsibilities doing interrogations and other types of intelligence work.

Whatever his work involved, Jack Neuman was very good at it. One citation states:

> As an interrogator, with the 5th Armored Division, Lieutenant Neuman performed his duties in a highly commendable manner. His ability, initiative, cooperative spirit and devotion to duty, reflect great credit upon himself and the armed forces.

After several months in the field, Jack earned his first promotion to First Lieutenant, effective October 23, 1944, by the command of General Eisenhower and undersigned by his Deputy Chief of Staff, Brigadier General R. B. Lord. Originally a temporary promotion, it subsequently became permanent. My father later received further recognition for his work on the front lines, earning the Bronze Star. This medal is awarded by the U.S. Army in recognition of heroic achievement, heroic service, meritorious achievement, or meritorious service in a combat zone. The recommendation for his medal first surfaces in a June 7, 1945 memo, and the award was formally presented in November 1945 by Brigadier E. W. Timberlake. The official recommendation outlines the case:

> First Lieutenant John. H. Neuman, while serving with the Army of the United States, distinguished himself by meritorious service in connection with military operations... He served with the 5th Armored Division as Interrogator from the Division's entry into combat to December 10, 1944 at which time he was injured and evacuated. Throughout this period, Lieutenant Neuman did outstanding work as an interrogator and obtained much valuable information

from the interrogation of Prisoners of War and civilians. During these interrogations, frequently done under fire, Lieutenant Neuman conducted himself in an exemplary manner which reflects credit upon himself and the military service.

Jack officially receiving his Bronze Star.

As a child, I knew all about his Bronze Star, which I recall seeing from time to time (it came in its own special box, which he kept in the top drawer of his bedroom dresser). I also recall a story that supposedly explained the medal, in which my father captured a bunch of German soldiers in the forest all by himself by convincing them they were surrounded by a larger group of Allied soldiers. This story is not mentioned in any of the surviving documents, and it could well have been one he made up to entertain his sons. And yet, this stunt isn't dissimilar to the exploits recounted by other Ritchie Boys in their memoirs. [22]

What is not documented is what it was like for my father to interrogate the people who collectively were responsible for his family's persecution and possible death. As a child growing up, I remember knowing that he played this role in the war, but I cannot recall how I learned about this or from whom. Perhaps it came from my mother, since my father never mentioned it. It was an unspoken family secret that he did some terrible things during his wartime service. I always thought this meant he physically abused and even tortured German prisoners, because this was the only thing I could imagine it might be, and it fit with what one saw in the movies. I also knew my father held a lot of anger inside him, which showed itself with terrifying force on rare occasions.

In the fall of 1944, the American forces (including Jack's IPW team) engaged with the German army in an extended series of fierce battles in the Hürtgen Forest, just east of the Belgian-German border. According to Wikipedia, this proved to be the longest battle on German ground during WWII, and the longest single battle the U.S. Army ever fought (exceeding 30,000 casualties). This was unusually treacherous terrain, including dense boggy forest, steep ridges and deep gorges, in which the Germans built strong defences with concrete bunkers, barbed wire, minefields, machine guns and steel-walled artillery emplacements. Complicating the advance was heavy overcast weather, which prevented the use of airpower to support the U.S. ground troops.

U.S. troops advancing during Battle of the Hürtgen Forest.
(West Virginia History OnView)

The terrible carnage resulting from this battle becomes clear in Bruce Henderson's book as he recounts the experience of Ritchie Boy Victor Brombert:

Victor would always remember the carnage he saw in the forest; the horror of mortar and artillery barrages; unrelenting shell bursts exploding in treetops, against which lying prone on the ground was no protection; torn and bloody clothing and body parts blown into the air and left hanging in tree limbs like Satan's laundry; armored tanks mired in thick mud and unable to move; soldiers too tired or too scared to leave their foxholes, even to relieve themselves. Men were cracking up, one combat medic told him. Some desperate soldiers were inflicting wounds on themselves, shooting their feet, toes or fingers so to get a medical evacuation.[23]

Almost at the very end of the battle, on December 10, 1944, my father was himself injured (described as "frozen feet") and quickly evacuated from the front. Records indicate he was a patient at the 97th General Hospital in the United Kingdom from December 6, 1944 through March 2, 1945, requiring a lengthy convalescence (as is common for this infliction). An early hospitalization record describes his condition as "Trench foot, bilateral, moderately severe, one small superficial ulcer, no gangrene." A subsequent clinical assessment two months later indicates he was still in the process of recovery ("bluish discoloration of the 4th and 5th toes of the left foot"), and that his feet were still sensitive after exercise or exposure to cold.

Jack was fortunate to eventually recover without the loss of any extremities. He was also very lucky to be away from the front at this time. One of the Ritchie Boys IPW units operating in the Hürtgen Forest was overrun by German troops, and two Jewish members were summarily executed once a German officer learned they were "Jews from Berlin."[24] And his evacuation took place just a few days before the start of the Battle of the Bulge, which proved to be the largest and bloodiest single battle fought by U.S. troops during WWII (suffering 89,000 casualties).

When Jack finally recovered from his injuries, he was no longer deemed fit to return to his previous role on the front lines. On March 2, 1945, he was designated for "limited assignment" as a "casual" at the HQ, MIS in Le Vesinet, France. This posting was temporary, as just a month later (April 8) he was re-assigned to serve as an Intelligence Officer (G-2 Documents Section) at the Supreme Headquarters Allied Expeditionary Force (SHAEF), first in Versailles and then Frankfurt.[25] He would serve out the rest of the war at a desk.

Throughout the time my father was in the Army (and even before he was sent overseas), he carried on a continuous correspondence with my mother (in her memoir she recalls writing him at least once a day the entire time he was away). None of their letters remain, but my mother held onto several dozen photos that he sent her from his training in the U.S. and then from Europe. Most of them are pictures of him, with annotations on the back that are sometimes just the general time period (1944-46), or the specific month and year it was taken. In some cases, the back of the photo identifies the scene or location, or who else is in the frame (where this includes Army colleagues, the back also includes an instruction "Not for publication" with another officer's signature). A few of the photos include messages of love and longing, such as one written by Jack on the back of a Christmas card dated December 8, 1945:

My Very Own Darling, On this – and definitely our last apart Christmas, my thoughts are with you and all I can think off (sic) is our next Christmas TOGETHER! I adore you darling; 1946 is definitely our lucky year and I just can't wait.
Your loving husband Jack.

With Jack now in central Europe and the war ending, his focus turned from intelligence work to finding out about the fate of his family (he had not heard from his father in almost four years). On June 13, he received instructions from a commanding officer at SHAEF to "proceed by military aircraft and/or Government motor transport to Pilsen for temporary duty of approximately nine (9) days." This is the dry record of what was to be an emotionally-charged trip.

My father didn't include in his brief memoir any mention of his return to Czechoslovakia, but he did write letters at the time, some undoubtedly to my mother, and also to his cousin Rose Oplatka and her husband Otto back in Chicago, three of which survive. The letters provide valuable insight into what he was up to, how he felt about his situation and what was going on in war-torn Europe. [26]

The first letter is dated May 26, 1945, from Versailles, where he was stationed at SHAEF Headquarters. He tells Rose and Otto he is "filled with obsession to get back to Plzeň," but is unable to leave because of the demands of the work. He laments the fact that he is no longer with the 5th Armored Division, when he operated independently and had his own jeep for getting around – and if he still did, he'd have already gone. But he then goes on to admit that:

> If I were quite honest with myself, I would have to admit that I actually dread the trip because I am afraid that the hope, still very strong in spite of odds, might be taken away from me.

All he can do at this point is intelligence work from afar, and he describes to Rose and Otto how he procured two 1944 Czech telephone directories (one for Prague and one for businesses across Bohemia). He spent hours ("none pleasant") poring over the listings to look for recognizable addresses. He cannot find a listing for his family's candy factory (but wonders if it's been renamed) or his family home in Plzeň. He does find the name of a business "Trojo," which belonged to the husband of his aunt (Rudolf Katz), but the proprietor listed (Steinmüller) is a former partner of Rudolf's and "an ardent Nazi even in 1939." He recalls meeting Steinmüller's wife, who despite being Jewish, "did not find anything wrong in greeting her customers with 'Heil Hitler'."

He also found listings for quite a few Jewish doctors in Prague (and one in Plzeň), which he understands to mean they were allowed to treat Jewish patients, concluding there must have been numerous Jews still in these places at the beginning of 1944. He notes there is no listing for Terezin, proving to him that the whole town was turned into a concentration camp for Jews (which at that time was still a rumour to the Allies, but was in fact the case).

The second letter is dated June 23, 1945 from Frankfurt, and written just after Jack returned from visiting Plzeň. As he reports succinctly to Rose and Otto, "Unfortunately my entire family disappeared to Poland via Terezin and only a miracle could bring anybody back." He then devotes most of the letter to what he is now doing to help those survivors he did find, in an itemized list (numbered 1 to 6). Item 1 involved organizing a "relief action" for the few Jewish friends of his and his parents who managed to return (he counts about 50 of the 3,500 who were deported). This involved sending food, cigarettes and old clothes to a central address. His motivation stems from having lost "all trust in the big welfare organizations, in Bohemia their activity is simply nonexistent."

Other steps he took involved setting up his own mail channel so that relatives overseas could write or send parcels to Czech family members in need, as well as delegating other local Czechs to search for specific relatives elsewhere in the country.

He writes that those who survived and returned to Plzeň were still wearing their concentration camp clothes, and have been given someplace to live (in their own homes, where possible), some furniture confiscated from the Germans, and additional food rations for a few weeks – but that this wasn't really sufficient without supplementing through the black market (which was less available to Jews, who no longer had the connections). He counsels Rose and Otto:

> I don't want to give anyone false hopes. It looks bad and if you want to know the end of most of our relatives go and see the film taken at the concentration camps after their liberation, but miracles do happen, and I hope that we shall find somebody at the least out of our big families. The majority of people back in Plzeň are from mixed marriages who had a much easier lot, the rest miraculous escapes. So far most of those returned are women.

But no miracle would happen for Jack, as none of his own immediate family or close relatives would ever return. Concentration camp records document that his father Adolf and brother Josef were transferred from Terezin to Auschwitz on January 18, 1942. Josef was killed on September 28, 1945 and Adolf shortly after on October 9.[27] The camp was liberated just a few months later, on January 27, 1945. As he closes, he says "I know so much – and yet so little of what we want to hear – it makes me want to vomit," then goes on to tell them, "Never before did I fully realize what that affidavit [Otto] sent me really did for me. I wish to thank you again – but words seem very inadequate about everything in the 20th century."[28]

First Lieutenant Neuman, August 1945.

The third letter is dated September 27, 1945 (from Berlin, where Jack was now stationed at the Berlin Document Center). This one starts out indicating that he would only write a short note, but it turns out to be a lengthy one. He reports that he is leaving for Plzeň the day after tomorrow and will also try to get to Tabor (where his cousin Gene's family is from), and hopes to have further news when he returns ("Perhaps miracles still happen").

He thanks Rose and Otto for packages received from them to be sent to other relatives, but goes on to admonish them for assuming they needed to instruct him to give the packages to Czechs and not Germans ("I must have certainly written a very strange letter to give you that impression [that I might give them to Germans]"). He also rebuffs their suggestion that he keep some of the received goods for himself, and that he is sending everything to others, even keeping his own cigarette consumption to a minimum in order to send them along to those in need.

The letter continues on a theme of addressing a misunderstanding in their correspondence. Jack writes that he found their most recent letter to him to be "pretty sharp" and that "perhaps I deserve it." The context is not fully clear, but it appears he previously wrote them about the situation in Europe, which prompted the "sharp" reply. In this letter, Jack tries to explain by saying:

> I have become quite disillusioned about the progress of things over here. But I really did not report to you on conditions in Europe, but on a couple of freak situations. Conditions here are too big a subject to take up in letters, so let's leave them until I get home."

But he then goes on to further explain that his previous comments about a military commander who played a key role at the end of the war (Andrey Vlasov) came not from him, but from a few Czechs from Prague he spoke to. He refers to Vlasov as a turncoat, but one who he says helped ensure Prague did not become another Berlin (perhaps suggesting it would have been bombed by the Allies and/or overrun by Soviet troops).[29] He writes about the prisoners of war he interrogated while in France who were Russians in German uniforms, conscripts whose only alternatives were to serve or be killed, and that they were of more help to the Allies than the German prisoners. He writes that perhaps Rose and Otto thought he had an "anti-Soviet flavor" in his remarks, which he dismisses. He goes on to say:

> I can't possibly write you all that is on my mind and I am sorry that I was so one-sided. However, there is not one country with the policy of which I could fully agree with. I did not turn isolationist, in fact I did not change. I am willing to cooperate with everybody, but seldom find the same attitude in others, including Americans.

He continues:

> It's really a farce that you should blame me for sympathizing with the Germans. You send them all to hell – however, that includes the 30,000 German Jews still left, those first opponents of Hitler who were found alive in the K2 camps and there are thousands of them, plus all those who are supposed to take over here – we aren't going to be here forever. They are all going to hell together, the victims and those who stood by and let this slaughterhouse go on.

He ends this theme by asking them "please don't write me again about my report on conditions in Europe," that they are just a few thoughts "out of a hat.[30]" Jack goes on to vent some frustration:

> Europe's problems used to occupy my mind quite a bit. Perhaps it's silly of me to even mention Germany. But I work here and on a pretty high level and I just often don't like how things are handled. I am realizing, however, that I got my own problems and that the world does not rest on my shoulders. I shall do my best to help those people from Czecho who survived, but I shall also have to look around for myself a little bit. I have a very insignificant job, yet no prospects of going home... I am really sick of this continent and very sick of the Army. If I were not an Intelligence Officer, I could have been home last December, yet my qualifications have not been utilized since [then]. I don't want to write a hard luck story, I am damn lucky to be still alive and I appreciate it.

He closes the letter by acknowledging it was quite a bit longer than he intended, but that what he wrote "did not even scratch the surface," and still hopes to make it home one day and talk with them further.

There is no surviving correspondence from Jack about his second trip to Plzeň. There is an Army order issued September 28, 1945 authorizing compassionate leave of 15 days, effective October 1, to allow him to travel to Pilsen and arranging for his accommodation at the American Red Cross, AEF Club or Army Corps Visitor Bureau. His stay was likely extended, as I have documents showing he deposited 75,000 Czech Crowns into his father's bank account with the Bank of Plzeň on October 23rd.[31] What these funds were intended for is unclear; perhaps they were needed to ensure his family home or business did not fall into arrears and be dispossessed.

Jack could find very little about his missing family members. In April 1945, he wrote to the Czechoslovak Jewish Representative Committee to inquire about the status of his father and brother. In a letter dated April 27, 1945, Professor Hugo Perutz, on behalf of the Committee, wrote back advising him that they checked their lists of persons to whom food parcels were being sent to Terezin, and found his father's name but nothing about Josef.

While Jack could do little about his father and brother, he continued to do what he could for relatives and other Czech Jews who had survived and returned to Czechoslovakia. This involved helping to locate missing family members, and arranging for parcels to be shipped from the U.S., with Joy providing support at that end. At that time, it was not possible to send parcels into the country without someone like my father serving as a middle-man. The scope of this effort becomes clear from the handful of letters he received from contacts in the U.S. and U.K. requesting his assistance and/or offering their thanks for his help. In a letter dated August 13, 1945, Max Kohn from Berwyn, Illinois writes:

> Dear Friend. Jack. Yesterday I received a Cable from Mrs. Dusek from Koterjrina [his niece] informing me her and her family are the only ones that came back. Although still disappointed, I still hope some of the others, especially the Boys from my brother are alive and will turn up someday somewhere. I wish to thank you very much for what you did for me, knowing you are so bussy (sic) and have to take care of so many requests, and especially I wish to thank you for the foresight you had in sending the money for the Cable. I am

enclosing a five dollar Bill and if it will not cover the expenses you had I will settle with you on your arrival in this country which according to events going on here should be soon.

But Jack would not be returning home anytime soon. On June 22, 1945, Lieutenant Neuman received new orders from Supreme HQ Allied Expeditionary Force (SHAEF) reassigning him and 16 others to the 6889th Berlin Document Center, which would turn out to be his final active duty posting with the U.S. Army.[32]

Underground vault at the Berlin Document Center.
(Allied Museum Berlin)

The Berlin Document Center (BDC) was set up by the U.S. provisional government in Germany to centralize and analyze Nazi documents for purposes of criminal prosecution and de-Nazification. The German authorities were well-known to be meticulous in the record keeping and documentation of practically everything, and the U.S. Army realized it needed to move quickly to recover documents before the evidence was destroyed or captured by the Soviet Army. According to a 1994 *LA Times* piece, intelligence officers went "from house-to-house, bombed-out ministry to bombed-out ministry, trying in each place to build enough confidence among shaken survivors to make them tell [them] where the evidence lay." And this yielded a tremendous amount of material, as one of them recalls, "We were overwhelmed by the mass of paper that came in, before we actually knew what happened."[33]

Other materials were recovered in the final week of the war when Michel Thomas, a Jewish concentration camp inmate who had escaped the Nazis and joined the U.S. Army Counter Intelligence Corps, received a tip about a convoy of trucks in the vicinity of Munich said to be carrying unknown, but possibly valuable cargo. Thomas went to the trucks' destination, where he discovered an empty warehouse filled with what turned out to be the complete worldwide membership files of the Nazi Party, on their way to be destroyed on the orders of the Nazi leadership in Berlin. The manager of the mill had promised to pulp the files right away, but ended up storing them in anticipation that they would prove useful to the occupying Allies (and perhaps as a way to curry favour with them).

The Berlin Document Center was established in a barracks-like complex surrounded by barbed wire, which sat above subterranean chambers that served as an extensive telephone surveillance center run by Field

Marshal Herman Goering (which they discovered to be filled with eavesdropping equipment, with the wires now cut). The Center ended up housing 75 million pages of documents, which were to be sorted, organized and analyzed for relevant information pertinent to the activities of the Nazi government over the preceding dozen years. The collection grew to house 11 million files on Nazi party members, covering about 85 percent of the party membership. This included not just those in Germany, but party members in the USA and other countries. As described in a *Philadelphia Inquirer* story from March 1946:

> There are more than 24,000,000 index cards and they unite to trace the tentacles of Nazism as those tentacles have wrapped themselves around the world. Each card records the name of a Nazi party member or sympathizer however he is, where he lives. The name of a student in Philadelphia is in the cards. And of a tailor in Detroit. And of a cashier in Addis Abba, a banker in Buenos Aires, a travelling agent in Shanghai, an electrical engineer in Glasgow. These persons and the millions like them are worried today, and with reason. No longer will they be able to keep their affiliations secret... For details not told by the index cards are produced by the paper mountain in the dusty loft. Such details as correspondence, photographs and signatures.
>
> Discovery of the master file of the Nazi party, together with its code book, is described by military authorities as the most valuable prize in documentary history, one destined to exert a profound effect upon humanity for generations to come.[34]

Jack at work.

This prediction, if sensational, was largely realized. The files held in the BDC provided the essential evidence for the Nuremburg trials, which took place between November 1945 and October 1946, in which prominent Nazi leaders were prosecuted for war crimes, including the Holocaust. Many of those accused did their best to deny their involvement in Nazi atrocities, but could not avoid the documented proof of their complicity, as recorded in signed membership cards, photos and genealogical records that were required to document one's Aryan bloodlines.

And the impact of the BDC extended well past the immediate post-war period. As recounted in a piece published in *The New Yorker* in 1984, "perhaps the most celebrated part it played was in the case of Josef Mengele," who managed to flee to South America and live out his days incognito. BDC files were used in 1985 to confirm the identity of his corpse.[35]

Given their language skills and expertise, it is no surprise that Ritchie Boys like my father played a prominent role at the BDC. The Center was staffed by about 120 American and 35 to 40 British military personnel, assigned to organize and analyze the documents, and provide abstracts of material relevant to other military units.[36]

There are just a few details about my father's work at the BDC, consisting of a handful of Army orders. These direct him (and others) to travel between Berlin and Furstenhagen Germany, mostly for unspecified reasons. One such order (dated January 10, 1946) is more specific. Lieutenant Neuman is listed as the commanding officer in charge of 22 Sergeants, Corporals and Privates, to "provide necessary security on train moving from Furstenhagen to Berlin in order to escort seven specified German Ministerial Personnel, who are to provide the necessary Divisional break-down of records" and are to remain in Berlin permanently.

The other Army documents from my father's collection include three typed statements in German that appear to be interrogation reports, two dated in January 1945 and the third in April of that year. The third is the most intriguing. It is titled "Erklaerung" (Explanation), given by Manfred

Rommel, the son of Field Marshall Erwin Rommel who was renowned for his wartime success leading the German Afrika Korps in Northern African campaign and later implicated in the 1944 plot to assassinate Adolf Hitler (for which he chose suicide as an alternative to being court martialed). There is no indication of what role my father may have played in organizing these reports, but it is certainly intriguing that he ended up with copies and held on to them.

As in his work as an interrogator, my father's work in document analysis was highly valued. A performance report covering the last quarter of 1945 (and signed by the BDC Commanding Officer, Lt. Colonel Hans Helm) gives First Lieutenant Neuman a score of 5.8 out of 7.0, with ratings of mostly 6s in each of 10 areas (his lowest ratings of 5 are for "initiative" and "force"). In a letter dated December 17, 1945, Colonel Henry C. Newton (ostensibly his commanding officer) writes to Colonel Helms to recommend my father be promoted to Captain. In making the case, he writes:

> Neuman has taken hold of things here in a very aggressive fashion and due to his unusual background, not only fits into our picture very well here but will continue to be a great help to any document installation. Inasmuch as he is down here working with me I feel more or less obligated to stress this matter with you inasmuch as you would have to initiate the recommendation.

Colonel Helms writes back a few days later to confirm that Lieutenant Neuman has "sufficient time in grade" and that he will submit a recommendation for promotion as soon as promotions are "'unfrozen' at this headquarters," and then does so on January 8, 1946. The recommendation was made under the condition that he was not under consideration for immediate relief from active duty, and had signed a "Retention on Active Duty" statement to this effect. So, it may well have been the case that this promotion was offered as consolation for keeping Jack in the Army a bit longer and delaying his return home. This promotion would not become official for another four months, when Jack was back in Chicago. The letter informing him of the promotion (dated May 7, 1946) is addressed to him at Joy's parents address, and states he is temporarily promoted to the rank of Captain MAC, "by direction of the President."

Needless to say, Jack was anxious to return home to Joy as soon as possible. On a standard administrative document providing personnel with an opportunity to indicate their preferences for continuing active duty (dated January 12, 1946), he checks off "Category V," which states, "I desire to be relieved from active duty at the earliest opportunity." On March 28, he finally receives orders relieving him from duty with the Office of Military Government for Germany (U.S.), and directing him (and others listed) to Belgium for release from active duty. After two years of service in the Army overseas and more than six years after he left his family home in Czechoslovakia, Jack Neuman, for the second time, boards a ship bound for the United States. This time, he is returning home.

Arriving back in the USA.

7

Starting Life Anew – Once Again

In June 1946, Jack Neuman returned home to the young bride he left behind two years earlier, and the couple soon departed for Cuba to enjoy a delayed honeymoon. Most of it was spent at Varadero Beach near Havana, at the time a favoured spot among Cubans, and what my mother described as "the most beautiful beach I've ever seen." It was off-season, and their hotel included only three other couples, all honeymooners, whom they got to know (judging from the number of photos taken). This was well before the Castro's communist revolution and when Cuba was a popular holiday destination for Americans.

Once back home, it was finally time for my parents to properly begin their life together. They spent the next few months living at the Hotel Plaza in downtown

Chicago, while searching for a suitable apartment. My mother describes this process as "unbelievably difficult" at the time, with apartments in such demand because of veterans returning home. She recounts the challenge in her autobiography:

> Just answering an ad was no good at all... So we developed a technique, which was eventually successful (if you can apply that term to the dump we found). Right after work each day I'd meet Jack at the Tribune Tower, where the next day's paper went on sale about 5:30 or 6:00. We'd stand in line and then immediately look at the ads and make a dash for a phone in the lobby – only to find them all in use. So we refined our technique: Jack would stand in line and I would commandeer a phone, either calling someone or pretending to, until he got the paper. Then we made a phone call and immediately made a dash to wherever the apartments were, by bus – we had no car yet. We got to see a lot of apartments that way, most of them awful. I can remember sitting in a living room with 15 other applicants, like a gruesome sort of party.

This is how they spent the next six weeks until they found a place that would take them. It was a one and a half room apartment in the red-light district (with at least one working girl in the building), but they finally had a place of their own. It was intended as a temporary place, but they ended up staying for three years.

Now decommissioned from active service in the U.S. Army, my father was now faced with figuring out what to do with his life. Many veterans opted to go back to school through the GI Bill, but he decided this wasn't for him.[37]

As my mother describes it, he felt his life had been on hold long enough and took seriously his role as the "man of the family." But, up to this point in his life, Jack never got around to developing any clear sense of career or work direction, as his young adult life had been focused on survival and responding to whatever opportunities presented themselves.

Jack and Joy on their honeymoon in Cuba. To their left are newfound newlywed friends Leon and Rosita.

Jack's early employment experience started with a couple of false starts. He began looking for work that would utilize what skills he had (mainly his language abilities), and focused on answering job ads and sometimes visiting employment agencies. He landed his first job at the beginning of August as a clerk at an import-export firm called Alsdorf A. J. Corporation. For some reason not explained, this job lasted only a week. Shortly after that he was hired as an Assistant Sales Manager at the Reliable Textile Company, only to be let go three weeks later so that the owner's son could take over the position.

Then, once again, Jack's good luck returned. The post-war period spawned the birth of the travel industry in the U.S., with new businesses starting up to promote leisure travel and help Americans figure out how to do it. In 1946, this was a nascent industry, but one my father thought might be a good fit with his language skills and European background. He responded to several ads for travel agents, including one with American Express. This resulted in a call for an interview, and turned out to be not with American Express, but with a small Chicago-area travel business called the Weiss Travel Bureau, where he would end up for the remainder of his career.[38]

The Weiss Travel Bureau was a family-owned business established by Alexander Weiss, located in the northwest part of Chicago. There is no extant documentation about its founding or operation, but its primary market appeared to be "ethnic" Americans interested in travelling back to their roots. Jack was hired as a multilingual bookkeeper. A bookkeeper, he writes, was "the one thing I could never be, nothing I added up ever balanced." But he found the office to be "fascinating even in those days of no travel," and he soon was given other work that made better use of his capabilities.

My father now had steady employment but he was not truly settled in this work. As he wrote, "I was still plagued with what would today be called an ethnic hangup. Am I going to spend the rest of my life ministering to Germans, or even Hungarians who are worse?" About 18 months later, he was offered what he describes as a better job with a Czech travel agency, and gave his notice. His boss, "wise old Mr. Weiss," didn't let go easily, and counselled Jack to think it over and consider that he might be better off staying with him, but Jack's mind was made up. Until the next day, however, when the Czech government was taken over by the communists and the border to the west was closed.[39] Very soon after, his prospective employer called to rescind the offer and he agreed to continue at the Weiss Travel Bureau. Once again, unanticipated external events would direct the course of Jack Neuman's life.

Now settled into his new life for two years, my father had a young wife, an apartment in the city and a stable job in the early post-war international travel business. What else was in his life? Neither he nor my mother ever spoke or wrote much about this time in their lives, but there are some clues. Still new to Chicago, Jack had no childhood friends – or few, if any, from his college years. He did have a sizeable number of Czech cousins who (apart from Gene Justic) settled in the Chicago area well before the war. This included his sponsors (Louis and Elsie Fisher, and their four children), as well as a few dozen other distant cousins. There was a well-established Czech community in the Chicago area, centred in the southwestern districts of Berwyn and Cicero. How close my father was to this family is unclear, although they undoubtedly provided him with social, as well as material, support in his early years in Chicago.

Extended family gathering on Thanksgiving, 1958. My parents are standing at the far left, with me in front wearing my favourite cowboy shirt (with the white fringe).

At some point around this time, the extended family started the tradition of gathering on Thanksgiving Day, a ritual I remember well from my childhood years. The event always started at midday with a traditional meal at a Czech restaurant somewhere on the southwest side, and then moved to someone's home for the remainder of the afternoon and early evening. These were large multigenerational gatherings, and the only times I saw most of my Czech relatives. Of course, everyone in the extended family was Jewish, but it would be all but impossible to know this, as everyone was thoroughly secular and, from what I could tell, had dispensed with their Jewish identity altogether.

Jack grew up in a secular Jewish home, but likely had some sense of his Jewish identity growing up, especially given the anti-Semitic treatment inflicted by other Czechs and Germans. But in his new country and among his thoroughly-secularized family relations, whatever Jewishness he had seemed to evaporate. This would have been reinforced by my mother, who also was brought up in a secular Jewish home and felt disaffected from her parent's Jewish cultural community (she never articulated what it was that offended her, but she felt compelled to distance herself and find an entirely new social milieu). As for my father, the only thing I ever recall hearing (likely from my mother) was that he didn't relate to American Jewish culture.

Among his Czech cousins, my father was closest to Louis and Elsie's youngest son Lester Fisher (who was roughly the same age). And for this reason, my "uncle" Les (but, in fact, my second cousin once removed) is the cousin I knew best growing up. He was a veterinarian and, like my father, had a notable WWII army experience (in his case, ensuring the health and well-being of General George Patton's bulldog and carrier pigeons). Les and his wife Beth became part of my parents' social circle, as recounted in a recent interview with Beth (this was among her most vivid early memories of my father in those early years). She recalls meeting my parents at a play, and hitting it off. And from there, they got together regularly, often at my parent's second apartment (much nicer than the first dingy one they managed to land). In later years, the two couples (now with children) would go in together to purchase a couple of sailboats, which became a summer pastime for both families.

I never saw my parents' second apartment in Chicago at 2052 North Halsted Avenue, but I recall hearing about it, as it was considered a big deal at the time. As described, it was spacious and featured a two-story living room, and furnished by my mother in what was just becoming the modern style of décor. I remember her talking about how wonderful it was, although they ended up living there for only a couple of years until their second child (me) arrived and they needed more space.

What I never knew about this time in my father's life is that he maintained his connection with the U.S. Army, serving in the Reserve for a number of years following his return to Chicago in 1946. This I discovered only recently from documents buried in the many paper files he left behind. It would explain why there was Army gear stored in a closet in our home: a couple of dress uniforms, a rifle and assorted military paraphernalia that would be of such fascination to young boys. I enjoyed the dress-up opportunities it afforded.

That's me in full army get-up, sporting
my father's U.S. Army cap.

Captain John H. Neuman was officially appointed to the U.S. Army Reserve on May 7, 1946 (very shortly upon returning to Chicago), "by direction of the President" as the correspondence intones. He was appointed as Captain in the MAC Reserve (Medical Administrative Corps, his original assignment in 1943), but was soon transferred to Military Intelligence, given his value to the Army was in intelligence and interrogation – WWII was now over, but the U.S. military was hardly demobilizing en masse, even with the onset of the Cold War to come a bit later. His initial assignment did not come with any specific duties:

He was instructed to "not perform the duties of an officer under this appointment until specifically so directed by competent orders."

Exactly what my father's duties and activities were in the U.S. Army Reserve is unclear. But he did hold onto official Army orders that reveal the following:

- November 9, 1950 – Reassigned to the 330th Military Intelligence Unit, Interrogator Detachment, designated as "(Czechoslovakian), suggesting the focus of his training and potential future assignments (with his home country now under Communist rule).

- February 5, 1951 – Assigned to "Organized Reserve Corps Field Training with the 330th Military Intelligence (MI) Detachment at Camp Ripley Minnesota for the period July 28 to August 11.

- February 26, 1951 – Assigned to active duty training (effective March 10), to a location simply indicated as Chicago, IL.

- July 3, 1952 – Approved by his commanding officer to be excused from attending a 15-day summer training camp.

My father ended his service with the U.S. Army Reserve on April 1, 1953, almost seven years after returning home from overseas service. In the official letter certifying his honorable discharge from Illinois Military District HQ, the Secretary of the Army extends his sincere appreciation for the service rendered to his country and the Armed Forces. His official "Separation Qualification Record" documents the details of his decorated Army career and lists the following service awards:

- Bronze Star Medal
- Good Conduct Medal
- European Theater Medal with 3 battle stars
- American Theater Medal
- Army of Occupation Medal with the "Germany" Clasp
- World War II Victory Medal

My father was now settled in the USA as a naturalized American, and no longer had meaningful connection to his country of birth, which was now firmly behind the Iron Curtain. His family was gone, and he had but a few relatives still in Czechoslovakia. But he still had unfinished business in doing something about his family's property that was confiscated during the German occupation. Of this part of my father's story, I heard very little from either of my parents. My mother once mentioned that my father spent several years trying to claim compensation and at one point retained a lawyer in London, but that little came of it.

What I never learned from them directly was eventually revealed in a set of folders holding documents left behind, a paper trail providing rich details of what transpired. Much of the information is in Czech, but several key documents were translated into English (noted as "Certified translations").[40]

The property in question was what my father inherited from his mother Emma, consisting of shares in two pieces of real estate. The first of these was the family's candy factory RINA in the "risske" suburb of Plzeň, which included gardens, a house, boiler house and coal shed. Emma owned one-quarter of this property, appraised in 1939 to be worth 125,450.75 Czech crowns.[41] The second property was a house and garden in the southern Czech town of Ceske Budejovice (described as in the Linz Suburb), and was likely inherited by Emma through her Bergmann family connections. She had a one-half share of this property, which was appraised at 63,420 crowns.

These details are outlined in an official court document specifying the direction of Emma's estate in the absence of a last will and testament (perhaps not surprising given the unexpectedness of her death). The document is dated November 6, 1939, six months following Emma's death and just a few weeks before Hanus (Jack) departed for the USA. What is most notable is the clause in which Emma's husband Adolf surrenders his rights to the inheritance in order to pass them in equal measure to his two sons, who were both minors at 18 and 12 years of age, respectively. Why did he do this? The only clue is that the document records Adolf's request that his sons be granted a reduction in inheritance fees, which by this point in the occupation may have been prohibitively high for Jews.[42]

The completion of this estate transaction (labelled as an "Order to Turn Over") was confirmed a few months later in a subsequent document dated February 10, 1940. By this time, Jack was now resettled in Chicago and in no position to claim his share. What these properties might have been worth to him is now impossible to estimate as the order stipulated that "each named heir pay the inheritance debts and as far as the inheritance suffices the expenses connected with the inheritance proceedings and state taxes."

The documentation picks up several years later with a letter sent to my father dated July 30, 1945, shortly after the end of the war, and with Jack stationed somewhere in Europe. The letter is from a lawyer in Plzeň (Dr. JUDr Matej Liska), who my father must have retained to search for his family's property. The letter is brief, but provides an update on his investigation, in which he confirms an inheritance from the death of his uncle Adam Bergmann and the property in Ceske Budejovice, which turns out to have been confiscated from Emma's cousin Olga Katz, who had the other half share in the property (Liska goes on to say he is trying to determine who currently has control of the property). There is no mention of the RINA property.

Two years later, Jack receives what must have been very welcome news. In April 1947, he receives two separate letters from the Czech Ministry of Labor Protection and Social Welfare granting his request for the return of his share of both properties inherited from his mother. The letters state that Emma Neumann "was and still is the registered owner of the aforementioned real estate," and that "for racial reasons the Germans confiscated ... the property and transferred it to the Management of Emigration Fund without changing the ownership and registration." The documents further note that Jack's father Adolf and brother Josef have not returned from concentration camp, and have a court appointed guardian (Emil Kvapli, Plzeň). It goes on to state "all participating parties claimed Jewish nationality," and that the applicant (Jack) "has actively participated in the fight against Nazism."

Less than two weeks later, an official hearing takes place before a court commissioner in Plzeň to formally establish the value of the RINA property, attended by court commissioner (Adolf Holub) and his secretary (Miloslava Oullkova), the appraiser (Architect Karely Mastny) and Jack's lawyer Matej Liska. The official report of this proceeding (for which, thankfully, there is a notarized English translation) includes a highly detailed description of the property, which the appraiser notes is in good condition, although became somewhat run down during the war, and assigns a total value of 812,807.10 Czech crowns (one-quarter of which is Jack's inheritance), based on the estimated value as of June 21, 1939.[43]

The former RINA factory property at Jikalce No. 4 in Plzeň, as it is today (street front and aerial view). (Google Street View)

What satisfaction this must have given my father upon receiving confirmation that he would recover something of his family's property and his own childhood. But, alas, it was not to be. Less than a year later, the communists took over the country, and over the next few years progressively curtailed the rights of property owners. Private property was never formally abolished by the country's Constitution, but policies and practices placed various limits on ownership and use. While the law provided for compensation of expropriated property, the process for claiming it was difficult and "so in reality there was no real compensation granted at all."[44]

The U.S. government was not prepared to challenge the Communist takeover in Czechoslovakia, having now demobilized much of its army in the European continent, and having little political capital to engage in further foreign conflicts. But, in 1949, Congress passed the *International Claims Settlement Act*, establishing a commission to determine the validity and number of claims by nationals or U.S. citizens based upon nationalization of American-owned property by Czechoslovakia on or after January 1, 1945. My father submitted a claim through this commission, which likely explains why so many of the relevant documents were translated and notarized in Chicago. For some reason, he did not file his claim until 1959, and then was likely spurred to action by an Amendment to the Act that year, which, among other changes, set a filing deadline of September 15 of that year.

The claims process took two years, which is partially documented in correspondence with the Commission. My father retained a lawyer (Clifford Rubin) to assist him with his claim. When this lawyer died suddenly in mid-1961, my father initially designated a second lawyer (Benjamin Leisser), but then soon after decided to handle matters on his own. By this time, Jack also submitted a claim for his father's share in the RINA property (also one-quarter of the value), and some of the correspondence addresses the Commission's questions about mortgages attached to the property. In a letter dated September 25, 1961, the Commission informed my father of its "proposed decision" on his claim, which amounted to total compensation in the amount of $13,140.15 USD for:

- Funds Jack had deposited in his father's bank account when he first returned in 1945 and was unable to withdraw later (75,000 crowns, at a rate of $1.00 for 50 crowns);

- His share of the RINA property and house in Ceske Budejovice (valued at $8,363.25); and

- Interest (6% per annum) covering the period January 1, 1945 to August 8, 1958.

The Commission denied his additional claims for inheritance from the estates of his mother (apart from the real property) and his uncle Adam Bergmann, citing the lack of sufficient documentation.

My father finally succeeded in winning compensation for his family's property, but it proved to be a small victory indeed. While the Foreign Claims Commission was authorized to determine rightful claims on confiscated property, it was not provided with the funds to pay these in full. The terms of compensation gave first priority to paying

$1,000 per claim (for amounts greater than this amount), and then further payments "from time to time" based on what might be available in the total compensation fund. Jack received the initial $1,000 in November 1961, and a further payment of $643.89 on December 5; less than 13% of his approved claim.

Years later, in May 1968, he wrote the U.S. Department of the Treasury about recovering further payments against his approved award (this time, with the help of a London-based attorney). Why he did so is unclear, perhaps it was because of changes in Czechoslovakia around the time of the Prague Spring. In its response (dated June 4, 1968), the Commission informed Jack that of the $113,645 in certified awards assigned to all eligible claimants of confiscated Czech property, only $8,540 (or 7%) was available from the relevant fund set aside for payment against these claims (of which my father received almost one-fifth of the total!). The fund was fully depleted, with no prospect of replenishment. Shortly after my father's death in 1976, my mother registered with the Commission as his sole beneficiary. In 1982, she received a brief letter from the U.S. Department of the Treasury confirming her being "entitled to the award," and that "a voucher will be issued soon for execution." So perhaps there was some further modest amount paid out in the end.

So ended my father's efforts to recover his family inheritance. Decades later, I took on the challenge, having little appreciation of what he had gone through or how it ended. In 2001, I heard about a small organization called Search and Unite, set up by London-based lawyer David Lewin to help people reclaim Nazi-era property, with a focus on Czechoslovakia. He connected me to a Prague-based lawyer (JUDr Alena Stumpova), who conducted a search of the RINA property and provided a report (along with a copy of a land survey of the property and a ream of title documents in Czech). She confirmed my father's one-half ownership as of 1947, and that the property was subsequently transferred to the ownership of the Czech state in 1971 under 1959 era government decrees. She explained that it would have been possible to make a restitution claim with the post-Communist Czech government, but the period for doing so lapsed in April 1991, and was only available to Czech citizens. She indicated the property was now owned in part by a private household and in part by a business called Jednota – Spotrebni druzstvo Tachov (a food store and possibly also a restaurant).

Another available route was through the Czech Endowment Fund for Victims of the Holocaust, and in 2001, I submitted an application for my father's lost property. This claim was disqualified because of the compensation my father received for the property through the U.S. Foreign Claims Settlement Commission (which affirmed compensation, but was never paid out in full). This proved to be the end of the road for ever realizing compensation for my Czech family properties. Of note is the curious omission of any reference in the surviving documents to my father's family home in Plzeň (the spacious apartment in the city center at 26 Veleslavinová Street). This home must have been owned by my grandfather, and he was likely forced to sell or give it away as his circumstances grew increasingly dire in the years prior to being deported to the camps. We will never know.

In the end, I was successful in recovering Czech family assets in the form of life insurance payouts. First, through the International Commission on Holocaust Era Insurance Claims, and the Class Action Insurance Settlement against Generali Insurance (through which my grandfather took out a policy in 1927). I learned about this Commission in 2001 through an advertisement in a local Ottawa newspaper, and was able to find Adolf Neumann's name on a list of policyholders published online by the Commission. A year or two later, a Tel Aviv-based lawyer contacted me about further outstanding insurance policies and, for a commission, successfully recovered payment for a portion of the life insurance policies of two of my father's uncles, Emil Neumann and Max Immergut.[45]

8

A World of Travel

The Englishman Thomas Cook is widely credited as the father of modern tourism, due to the extensive business he built in the 19th century and which continues today. But international travel was not a common experience for most Americans until after WWII. The rising affluence afforded by the post-war economic boom – along with the expansion of transatlantic air travel, made convenient through jet aircraft in the late 1950s – enticed a new wave of middle-class Americans to visit Europe and other places they knew only by reputation, the media and literature. Included in this wave was a significant number of Americans with European roots who could now travel back and connect with extended family and ancestral roots as the continent was recovering from the devastation of world war. Thus began the contemporary international travel industry, and what many consider the "golden age of flight" for those who could afford it.[46]

The emergence of international travel for the middle class underpinned the business of the Weiss Travel Bureau, located near many of the city's concentrated ethnic neighbourhoods, especially those with Eastern European roots. Jack Neuman's job titles were both "manager" and "travel agent," and his official duties were numerous:

- Plan travel itineraries to all parts of the world;
- Make reservations;
- Process travel documents;
- Keep informed of travel regulations and restrictions;
- Conduct tours and excursions to Europe; and
- Supervise the work of 12 employees.[47]

He also gave lectures to other travel agents. Correspondence dated December 15, 1954 from the Midwest Chapter of the American Society of Travel Agents (ASTA) confirms an upcoming lecture he is to give the following January as part of the "basic course of study" for Chicago-area travel agents. His lecture is titled "Europe IV: Transportation," in which he is to:

Give the student an overall picture of the transportation within Europe. This discussion will cover air, rail, bus and steamship service as well as sightseeing on a local and regional basis. There will be an emphasis on the differences and similarities of service in various countries. There will also be some discussion of typical sightseeing patterns in some important cities as well as out of town excursions and such interesting inter-city trips as Rome-Florence and Rapallo-Nice.

How my father acquired the knowledge and experience by which to give such a lecture, based on just a few years in the industry, is an intriguing question. The most likely answer is that he bluffed his way through it, as he often did when faced with a situation for which he wasn't fully prepared.

Undated photo of Jack at his desk, with an unidentified man.
This is the only known photo of him at the office,
where he spent so much of his time.

Jack was well-suited to the travel business, and he almost certainly played an essential role in the company's success. He writes that he was well-paid, but also feeling antsy in a managerial role and "looking for my own company." And then, as happened yet again at a key moment in his life, out of nowhere the world opened up for him. In 1956, company owner Alexander Weiss suddenly died, and left the firm to both his son Herbert and my father. This came as a complete surprise to everyone, and my father briefly writes about it in his memoir almost 20 years later: "I was speechless and still am, the age of fairytales is dead isn't it? It never existed anyway, what can I say?"

Herb Weiss and Jack Neuman, co-owners of
Weiss Travel Bureau. (undated photo)

Now as co-owner of the Weiss Travel Bureau, my father found his life's calling and it became the center of his life until the end. What this meant to him is revealed in what he writes in 1973:

I have always loved my work and still do. I have looked at it
more as a teaching position. When I started Americans did
not travel – perhaps the upper crust, but not the ordinary
people. The only ones travelling abroad were the "Ethnics"

and I was one of them and looked for ways to make it easier and cheaper for them. And a whole world to show the native American! Forget the fact that I have not really seen it myself, usually I know more about a country or area before I visit it than after I have been there. After all, mine is only one opinion and even Herb and I don't agree on the best way to see a country. Yet here I could base my advice and help on the opinion of many.

It was not an easy business to run. As the industry evolved, new types of players like credit card companies, charters and travel clubs entered the market to serve the growing appetite for international travel, making it increasingly difficult for small service-based agencies like Weiss Travel to compete. Travel services were also subject to unexpected and costly disruptions in the form of new government regulations, as well as the outbreak of revolutions and other forms of regional conflict. They had to adapt. My father writes that, at one point, when it looked like their business might get wiped out by charter companies, they fought back by putting together their own "phony" travel club to hold onto clients. But this was not how my father liked to do business, and he expresses mixed feelings about what it took to keep the company afloat:

> ... neither one of us [himself and his partner Herb Weiss] like to do anything which is not proper, or legal, or not on the 'Up and up" or whatever one would want to call it. We are uncomfortable doing anything which we know is not strictly according to the rule and regulations and the fact that everybody does it does not make us feel any better. Also, we like to help people with their travel arrangements whether we make a big profit out of it or not and we

are finding more and more, that this is a true luxury we don't seem to be able to afford. Nowadays the money lies in shoving people into groups and prepackaged travel whether they like it or not, more like selling refrigerators than travel and we don't like it. I know that I don't like it and it bothers me a great deal.

It was also a challenging business to run. Jack and Herb made for good partners, and they treated the staff more as family than employees. But this sometimes backfired. The company's bookkeeping was done by hand (as was standard practice at that time) and, for many years, they left the accounting to a bookkeeper (a woman who I recall was quite friendly with me). It was only after she left that they discovered she had embezzled quite a bit of money over the years, which clarified why they never seemed to have as much money as they thought they should have. They learned a hard lesson and invested in computer bookkeeping, which was then becoming available. Employee theft also came in the form of someone making off with blank airline tickets stolen from the company safe.[48]

And even the part of the business my father enjoyed most – helping clients realize their travel dreams – came with its own headaches. Providing travel services at the time was hands-on and involved making a multitude of coordinated bookings for travel, accommodations and sightseeing. Clients could be demanding and were often unreasonable in their expectations. Jack Neuman was exceptionally skilled at managing these challenges so that his clients enjoyed their travel experience. He often made himself available to his clients during their travels, and sometimes took calls from them at home when emergencies cropped up.

Jack with other travel executives departing
Chicago on a new El Al flight to Israel in 1960,
as guests of the Israeli Government. (El Al)

Keeping his clients happy took its toll on him; as a child, I remember how our family dinnertime conversation would often feature my father complaining about this or that difficult client. Eric recalls one night at dinner when our father asked if either of us might be interested in entering the business and eventually taking it over. My brother's immediate response was "no way, every night you come home and complain about work," to which he apparently replied, "What do you mean? I love my work."

I have no memory of this or what I may have said at the time, but I felt exactly the same way as Eric; my father did not look to me like a good role model when it came to career choices.

Of course, part of my father's work involved his own travel, and he did a lot of it over the course of his career. Much of the time he travelled overseas by invitation from airlines, destinations and governments looking to attract American tourists (known as "fam tours"). Most destinations were emerging tourist hot spots, but one such trip was different and took on special meaning for Jack, as it took him back to his native country. In May 1959, he became one of the first Americans to travel as a private citizen behind the Iron Curtain, visiting Poland and Czechoslovakia.

This was a 10-day all-expenses paid trip offered to travel agents in the U.S. and other countries by Air France as part of its inaugural Paris to Warsaw service. The original itinerary included only Poland, and my father almost backed out, but in the end decided to go. Once in Poland, he then managed to slip into Czechoslovakia. The trip itself was remarkable, but even more so because he wrote about it in a four-part series that was published in the *Victor Press,* of Victorville, California (published August 6 - 27, 1959).[49]

Part of a fam tour on the ocean liner MS Gripsholm.
(Swedish American Line)

The first of the four articles tells of his visit to Warsaw, and he writes that his arrival "was the first shock," finding the city to be "completely destroyed and then left to stagnate... and gives the impression that the war has been over only about a year or so." He notes that, even having seen the bombed cities of England and Germany during and right after the war, he was not prepared for what he found in Warsaw (this was 14 years after the end of the war).

On his last day, he visited the remains of what was once the ghetto and "realized the destruction in Warsaw itself was nothing compared to what happened here ...

> The area of the ghetto seemed about equal to the Chicago loop and all of it was [completely] levelled to the ground. And, because of the rubble, the ground was about 10 feet higher than in the rest of Warsaw. Today, about half this area is still level. The other half is filled with new apartment buildings, many built right on top of the rubble.

He writes further about what he describes as "an unhappy and unfortunate city." But he later goes on to say that, despite all of the destruction, the feeling in the city is "pretty good. The people are hopeful and full of spirit."

After three days in Warsaw and the vicinity, the travel group leaves for the provinces and Jack stays behind to obtain a visa to Czechoslovakia. He doesn't provide details of this effort, but ends up flying to Prague the next night without a visa. He arrives late at night and the airport officials are unsure about what to do with him, but he gets lucky as he happens to encounter a welcoming committee composed of other officials from the airline and the Czech government travel agency (Cedok). After some waiting and suspense, he is given a one-day visa, which the next day he manages to extend to cover four days.

My father was likely one of the first American citizens (and expatriate Czechs from the West) to be allowed into this Iron Curtain country, which undoubtedly happened because Cedok saw him as potentially valuable in promoting tourism from the USA. But he soon comes to second guess his bravura. As he recounts:

I was very proud of myself and convinced that I had found the magic formula for dealing with the Communists. But I would now be much happier if they had booted me out of the country the first night.

First of Four Exclusive Articles: A Private Citizen Takes a Look Behind the Iron Curtain

The author, a friend of the editors, owns a travel bureau in Chicago. He recently returned from a "behind the Iron Curtain" trip to Poland and his native Czechoslovakia. This is the first of four articles on what he saw there. Mr. Neuman, now an American citizen, served with Army Intelligence during World War II.

By Jack Neuman

Part I

I have no business leaving the office in May even for a few days as it is our most important month. But when I received an invitation for a 10-day free trip to Poland and Czechoslovakia, I just could not refuse.

For their inaugural flight from Paris to Warsaw, Air France invited about 20 travel agents from the United States and 30 from the rest of the world. When I found out a week before departure that we would be visiting only Poland, I was already too deeply in to back out.

The arrival in Warsaw was the first shock. The city was so completely destroyed and then left to stagnate for so long, that even now — after about three years of feverish rebuilding activity — it gives the impression that the war has been over only about a year or so.

Ruined City

I have seen the bombed cities of England and Germany during and right after the war, but that did not prepare me for this. I was told that from a prewar population of over a million and a half, there were only about 50 people left there at war's end. And I believe it.

On my last day, I visited what used to be the ghetto and realized that the destruction in Warsaw itself was nothing compared to what happened here. The area of the ghetto seemed about equal to the Chicago loop, and all of it was completely levelled to the ground. And, because of the rubble, the ground was about 10 feet higher than in the rest of Warsaw!

Today about half this area is still level. The other half is filled with new apartment buildings, many built right on top of the rubble.

Monuments

At the edge of the ghetto stands a monument to the Jews who fought the Germans in the ghetto uprising. They did such a good job of building this, that it is already being repaired! It was taken apart and I did not really see it.

More impressive was an older but simpler monument —a large iron manhole with a short inscription: "The exit from the ghetto sewers."

Jack Neuman

If you read Hersey's "The Wall" or even the recent "Exodus," you can imagine how I felt standing there. I had traced a lot of uncles, aunts and other relatives as far as Warsaw.

An unhappy and unfortunate city. While the Jews were being slaughtered, the Poles stood idly by. And when later the Poles staged an uprising, at a time when the Russians had reached the other side of a lazy, shallow river at the eastern edge of the city, the Russians stood idly by allowing the Germans to finish their ghastly project.

Depressing Town

Now the city is populated almost exclusively with Poles from the provinces who have the most amazing "joie de vivre." In this shabby, depressing, sickening town, where all that is now being built (after they painstakingly restored a medieval looking main square in the old town so it would again look as it did in the middle ages) are ugly apartment buildings, one just like the other, and where people move into these buildings long before they are finished, these same people go about their daily business with enthusiasm!

They even smile and joke. Try to find that somewhere behind the Iron Curtain outside of "mother Russia"!

They criticize the Russians, tell jokes about them ("Now this ugly building is a gift from Russia to the Polish people. They supplied the blueprints. All we had to do is supply the labor and materials.") and tell you how beautiful Warsaw will look when it is all finished.

Hopeful Spirit

Once you get used to the destruction all around you and the raw looking new buildings (they haven't got the time or the materials to finish them and most of them are built of reconditioned brick not covered with anything), the feeling in the city is pretty good. The people are hopeful and full of spirit.

It was not always like this. It dates back only to the mild uprising in 1956 and the beginning of the new Gomulko regime. For reasons unknown, they are still allowed some private enterprise. The black market in dollars (actual greenbacks) and gift certificates from the USA, flourishes.

In a village a few hours drive away, I attended a ceremony in a Catholic church filled to overflowing and more

Continued on page 5

Page 1 of Jack's first published piece in the Victor Press about visiting Czechoslovakia in 1959.

What he finds in his country of birth, since first returning after V-E Day in 1945, is depressing and must have caused much sadness. Unlike Warsaw, Czechoslovakia experienced little physical damage. The country's economy seemed to be humming, but he notes:

The people are shabbily dressed and walk about listlessly with a dull expression. Nobody laughs, nobody talks much. There is very little automobile traffic, even in the main streets of Prague where it used to look like State and Madison before the war.

The final three parts of the newspaper series focus on what Jack learns about life in Communist Czechoslovakia, as told to him by the few friends and others prepared to open up to a foreigner. He concludes the oppression is primarily economic, as most people struggle to make ends meet under a strictly regulated economy that rules out free enterprise. Anyone who previously employed workers is labelled "socially unreliable" and relegated to menial jobs that pay very little. Doctors are no longer allowed to offer care outside of the government system, which now pays them by the number of patients they see. House calls are no longer allowed, even for emergencies (which might still happen under the radar and at great cost and risk to all parties). Of Jack's experience in the country, he writes, "I felt I was in a concentration camp. And it looks it too."

The people he speaks with are by no means supportive of the current regime or happy with the state of their country, but resigned to making the best of what is possible. He meets one "dyed-in-the-wool Communist" (a Cedok guide), who claimed he read *The New York Times* every day and insisted that my father did not know the true reality of the USA, being "a poor victim of our capitalist press." The rant stopped only when my father explained that he owned his own business and enjoyed a comfortable lifestyle; but later he wondered if this fellow concluded he was either a liar or related to the Rockefellers.

Jack writes about the difficulties Czechs face should they want to leave the country. Single people are simply not given permission to do so (he mentions the Czech representative for Air France in Prague who had never visited the corporate home office in Paris). The government sometimes allowed individuals with families to travel abroad alone, provided their families remained behind as collateral. He writes about one such person that got off a plane in Montreal and asked for political asylum, doing so despite leaving his wife and children behind.[50]

During his brief stay, Jack was able to visit his hometown of Plzeň, which must have been a difficult experience. He writes about the apartment house where he grew up:

> ... which survived the war without a scratch [but] now looks as if the battle had just passed it. Big pieces of plaster are down on the outside, and it looked so dreadful I fled before I could muster up the courage to go in. The only thing well preserved was my mother's grave (appropriate?) and I am now trying to find out who is looking after it.

The trip was successful in that he made it into the country and returned safely. But the end result put him in a quandary. As he writes:

And now I find myself in a strange position of being a representative of Cedok, a tourist representative of Czechoslovakia and hence registered with the [US] State Department as an 'agent of a foreign power' and am supposed to sing the praises of Czechoslovakia and send them as many tourists as I can!

He goes on to say:

I sat down quietly with my conscience for a while and thought about this dilemma. When I get somebody in my office who is interested, I tell them about the same as I am telling you.

My father concludes by saying the only people who do travel to Czechoslovakia are those with close relatives. He states that every American should go and "take a good look," but since he returned there haven't been any "real tourists" who have done so.

My parents partaking in recreation at a dude ranch in Colorado. (1947)

Not all of my father's travels were for work, or at least just for work. Over the last three decades of his life, he travelled the world extensively as a tourist (often with my mother, and on a few occasions with us children), in many cases fully or partially paid by the airlines and destinations who counted on my father's business. My mother was very keen to travel, and I recall her mentioning once that she agreed to have children only on the condition that they continue to travel. I don't recall hearing much about my parents' travels growing up, nor did either of them write much about it. But they did leave behind a rich photographic legacy in the form of several thousand 35 mm slides, many of which are labelled or annotated as to date and location.

Jack and Joy were especially active in their travel in the years before my brother Eric and I came along. This included trips to a Colorado dude ranch (1947); camping in the northwoods of Minnesota (1948); a European tour that included Switzerland, the French Riviera and Italy (1949); South America (Panama, Peru, Chile, British Antigua) (1950); and then Italy again (Sicily, Florence, Amalfi, Capri, Assisi) (1952). In 1961, my parents took our first family vacation, most of which was spent on a then as yet undiscovered island of Mallorca (no doubt because my father was keen to explore its potential as a travel destination.

Jack at the helm of a windjammer on Lake Michigan. (1953)

Jack posing on a donkey somewhere in the Caribbean
or South America. (undated photo)

Once children arrived, travel became more family-oriented. This included ski trips to Colorado and Michigan, a driving adventure to South Dakota (featuring a visit to the Rosebud Indian Reservation) and several trips to Mackinac Island, Michigan.[51] By the time Eric and I were teenagers in the late 1960s, my parents once again began travelling overseas, to Europe, South America and the Caribbean. In 1972, they were among the first tourists to visit the Galapagos Islands.[52]

Jack and Joy on a cruise, with another couple, somewhere south in the early 1950s.

Jack and Joy in Amsterdam, in the late 1960s.

My brother and I at the Rosebud
Reservation in South Dakota (1963).

9

Family Man

Once Jack had established an American life with a wife, a home and a career, he was ready to begin a new chapter with the arrival of children, starting with my brother Eric in 1952 and me two years later. Having children was by no means a foregone conclusion for our parents. My mother grew up with the firm conviction never to have children, "only puppies," she would write in her autobiography. She goes on to say that this determination "stayed with me as an adult, and I felt so strongly about it that I actually considered the possibility of suicide should I become pregnant." Where this intention originated isn't stated, but Joy struggled with psychological demons throughout her life, and firmly believed she had an unhappy childhood; perhaps she just convinced herself that parenting and children wasn't for her.

But as determined as Joy may have been on the matter of children, her perspective changed through the process of therapy. She placed herself under the treatment of Dr. Irene Mead, who had studied with the illustrious Dr. Carl Jung in Switzerland, and who herself raised five children while completing her training. Joy met with Dr. Mead once or twice a week over five years and later acknowledges "it literally changed my life." Over time, she progressed through stages from the 'suicide option', to accepting the possibility of having children, to finally wanting them.[53] And, she writes that Jack was "with me all the way, in terms of how I felt. He never attempted to pressure me in the least, and supported me however I felt." She also extracted from him one firm condition: that having children would not mean the end of their life of travel.

The family home on 1724 Isabella Street in Evanston, IL.

The city apartment on Halsted Street, as wonderful as it was for entertaining, was less than ideal for life with small children. There was no private outside space, and a second summer of hot humid weather convinced my parents to find a proper house out of the city.

As with many growing families at that time, the place to go was the suburbs, and for those who could afford it, the pleasant North Shore communities near Lake Michigan. Jack and Joy focused on Evanston, just north of Chicago, which they preferred as "the best bet because it had an excellent school system and was the only heterogenous suburb on the north side." In August 1953, they moved to 1724 Isabella Street, on the northern boundary of Evanston, which would become the family home for the next quarter century. It was an unusual house, in terms of its design (inspired by the prairie style of Frank Lloyd Wright), which my mother chose to decorate with walls painted in distinctive shades of pink, green and blue, together with modern art. It suited my parents' unconventional tastes.

What was Jack Neuman's life like as a family man? From my own recollections, it was about the time and energy he put into his work and business. My father worked long hours, officially five days a week but often six, and typically not arriving home for dinner before 6 p.m. on most weekdays, and after 9 p.m. on Thursdays. My mother wasn't happy with this schedule and pushed him to bring some of his work home so he didn't have to spend as many hours in the office. In response, my father set up a home office in their bedroom, which was spacious and could easily accommodate a good-sized desk, a filing cabinet and other office accoutrements.

Jack relaxing on the back patio.

With the time and effort devoted to his business, Jack had limited time for other pursuits and hobbies. Unlike many men, he had little interest in team sports, either as a participant or a fan. He watched the occasional hockey game on TV, and once took me to a game in Chicago featuring the national amateur U.S. and Czech national teams.54

The one sport Jack came to love was sailing. It's not clear if he had any sailing experience in his youth, but he enjoyed sailing trips prior to starting a family, and in 1961 got his sons involved during the family trip to Mallorca. We then became a sailing family, starting with a dinghy (dubbed the "Stone Cork" because it was so ugly and slow), and later moving up to larger more seaworthy sailboats, in partnership with cousin Lester Fisher and his family.

Jack and Eric sailing off Mallorca. (1961)

Les worked for the Chicago Park District (as Director of the Lincoln Park Zoo), which offered him preferred access to one of the difficult to get moorings in a city harbour. The first of these was a Swedish-made 28-foot Kings Cruiser, a beautiful wooden sloop that required considerable upkeep. Jack loved it, and I remember spending days at the boat yard labouring at the not so fun maintenance that was required to keep wooden boats afloat. Several years later, we moved on to a slightly smaller fiberglass boat (Rhodes 19) that was much easier to maintain, and featured a roomier cockpit for family members and friends. Eric and I became sailors in a big way, and this pastime occupied our summers throughout adolescence.

The other family sport was downhill skiing. Jack likely learned to ski in his youth, and in 1963 our parents decided to give downhill skiing a try; this was at a time when the sport was just on the cusp of becoming widely popular in the U.S. That year, we took a family ski trip to Colorado (taking a sleeper car train from Chicago to Denver), followed by subsequent trips to northern Michigan. These were among the few family travel opportunities for Eric and me as small children.

Photography was also one of Jack's casual recreational pleasures. He sported a high-quality 35mm Leica camera, and made good use of it while travelling, and sometimes at home. This was not always appreciated, at least by me, when he would decide to do a photo shoot with his children at some nearby location (the evidence can be found in my sullen face in some of the surviving photos). Today, of course, I appreciate the effort he made to take so many pictures (almost all as 35mm slides), and to hold onto them for me to now treasure.

Jack making a dramatic entrance in the Morton Grove Playhouse production of *The Man Who Came to Dinner*.

When Eric and I were small, my parents' social lives seemed to revolve around a few couples, and more occasionally with extended family. In those early years in Evanston, they were part of a local area drama club that would put on plays with their friends.

Over this period, they also hosted Saturday brunch parties at our home, which I've been told included alcohol.[55] I don't have memories of my father having close male friends, with whom to go off to do "guy" stuff; but perhaps I simply wasn't paying attention to something like this. He was close to his cousin Les Fisher, and our families became closer when we shared sailboats. He kept in touch with Gene Justic (with whom he travelled to the new world), but for the most part, our contact with his extended family of Czech relatives in the Chicago area was limited to the annual Thanksgiving get-togethers.

As a couple, Jack and Joy seemed to get along well, as I imagine it may have seemed to most observers. My parents shared a full life together, but had very different personalities. My mother described one of my father's great gifts as having "an easy going nature which enabled him to get along with people," and this was likely an essential trait in getting along with her. Joy, by contrast, had a harder edge; she was by nature a judgmental person who could be outspoken and at times difficult to be around. And she had clear opinions about my father, as he describes in his memoir, especially as it pertains to what she saw as his indecision:

> Which brings me to my 'modus operandi' – the way I act, or properly said, I don't act but only react. Joy cannot accept this and I understand now that she considers this a terrible weakness, but how could I act otherwise? The force of destiny described above is just the start...
>
> She is a person who feels a need to choose a course and follow it, be decisive... She must firmly believe that my problems at the office would be over if I only acted decisively too. I have too much work to do? Hire more people. European business is on the way down? Send them to Hawaii. Not enough room? Find a bigger place. Business down? Advertise... Joy knows that she could not last a week at my job, but seems to have no confidence in me handling

it either. How can I convince her? Am I really so weak that she cannot have confidence in me and all I have written are just excuses?

As he nears the conclusion of his writing, he laments:

> If that woman of mine could only relax a little. It now seems that Joy is the only one and the only thing in my life I never solved.

It was my mother's conviction that problems could be tackled head on that explains her lifelong dedication to therapy and self-improvement, which took her down many roads in search of answers to her personal demons. And it was Joy who pushed my father, just a few years before his death, to start down the same path and for the first time to begin to explore his own psychological wounds.

As a parent, my father wasn't as present as my mother was, given that he spent so much of his time and energy on his business. We did not spend a lot of time together on things like sports, outings and travel (we took the occasional family vacation, though he never took Eric or me along on any of his business-related travel). He did, however, bring Eric and I along with him when he visited his office on Saturdays; he would find us tasks to do such as stamping travel brochures with the company stamp, sometimes paying us a few cents per brochure for our effort.

To be honest, for much of my childhood I didn't miss father-son time because I generally felt uncomfortable around him. What I remember best is how I didn't look forward to the days of the week when he wasn't at his office (Wednesdays and Sundays).

Our relationship was a difficult one for both of us. I didn't understand why at the time, and wonder if it was in part because we were alike in some ways. When I was young, I resented the fact that my father wasn't an 'American dad' like the other dads in the neighbourhood and the ones I saw on TV. I wanted to fit in, and it didn't help that my father spoke with a bit of an accent (he pronounced the "w" in "weather" with a "v" sound, which would always irritate me). He would often ask me to do things in a way that I found aggravating, like he was treating me as a younger child than I was.

My father had a pleasant disposition most of the time, but on rare occasions his temper would get the better of him and he would explode with anger in response to something I or Eric might do; this I found truly terrifying. Eric recalls one time when my father got so mad at me for something or other, he chased me the full length of our living room and tried to kick me, with me just managing to avoid blows by running upstairs. My mother often tried to mediate this father-son tension, usually with mixed success. My father and I would enjoy rare moments of bonding when teaming up against my mother during some trivial argument.

Father and sons enjoying a happy Christmas moment. (early 1960s)

There was an underlying family dynamic in which I was put in the role of scapegoat – often seen as the problem and source of whatever tensions might be taking place. In hindsight, I think this may have been in part because I was the lone "younger sibling" in a family of older siblings (both of my parents were the older of two siblings of the same gender). My response was to assert myself as best I could, and this didn't usually go over well.

My father was also frustrated with his relationship with me. And perhaps he found it especially difficult because he had such a different and much closer relationship with his own father (as he remembered it, anyway). His feelings show through in his short memoir in the one place where I am featured:

And Keith? We thought of him as a real bastard, knows what he wants and goes after it. Really decisive – and Joy should like that, but she is not too happy either; especially since she does not always approve.

By the time he was writing these words (in 1973, by which time I was 19 years of age), our relationship had improved noticeably. He goes on to write:

Keith may have been tailor-made for this world, but this summer I have detected signs of mellowing. He is not such a bastard after all, and has shown consideration for others. I have had my problems with him, but after talking to him some this summer, they seem not to be because of substance, but because of form... I believe that both boys will manage, each in his own way and I am absolutely confident in calling Joy dead wrong if she thinks that the boys resent me or hate me or whatever it is she believes.

While this uncomfortable dynamic dominated my childhood relationship with my father, I later came to appreciate him more fully as a person in his own right. He was a warm and loving person, and the more affectionate of my parents. He was generous and giving (as was my mother) to my brother and I throughout our childhood and beyond. They provided for our every need (apart from a few minor exceptions like a colour TV when this was becoming a thing), supported us in almost every activity or adventure we wanted to undertake, and offered new ways to expand our horizons. My father had a good sense of humour and would sometimes make up stories just to kid us (something he may have learned from his father). One time, when I was young, he convinced me that the hot and cold faucets in a basement sink were reversed because that was how it was done in Czechoslovakia.

And my father was – as I can now appreciate – a wonderful role model. Against the predominant image for men of the time, my father was anything but a dominating male patriarch. He was certainly masculine, but never overbearing, and treated women with respect and at times deference. Part of my father's appeal may be what is sometimes described as old-world European charm.

Both of my parents were principled and did their best to live by the values my mother would later define as:

> truth, honesty, respect for others no matter their color or nationality, an ethic of hard work and the unimportance of money beyond what is necessary for a comfortable life, and the importance of treating others fairly.

And my parents were unequivocally progressive in their politics, from Adlai Stevenson onward. There is indeed a lot of myself in both of them, and I am thankful for that.

In my father's American life, it was never clear to me (or perhaps to anyone else) what he held onto from his childhood in Czechoslovakia. He rarely spoke of it. The story of his childhood and parents was known in our family only in the vaguest of terms.

What remained invisible was the bigger story about my

father's Jewish background and his connection to the Holocaust, and the true reason for his exodus to America. It was common in the mid-twentieth century for survivors and their families to leave this story alone, as it seemed to be case that others weren't interested in hearing about it. I expect my parents saw no reason to tell their children, and perhaps they felt they were protecting us in some way. This part of our family past was simply missing, and like most Americans we focused on the present and future. So, when my father's cousin Dita Vidar (nee Katz) and her family from Israel came to the Chicago area for a year in the early 1960s, the concentration camp tattoos appearing on her arm and that of her husband Max were no more than curiosities; I knew what they were, but didn't make any connection to my own family.

Jack maintained a connection with his native country through his relatives in the Chicago area (and a few still in Czechoslovakia) and his preference for the Pilsner Urquell, the famous Czech beer from his home town.[56] I imagine it was painful for him to think about his lost family and life, and what had become of his country under Communist rule. It wasn't something I remember him ever talking about.

Growing up, I understood that I had a Czech background, and at one point developed a more emotional connection through music. In junior high school, a class assignment required me to select a piece of classical music to write about. This led me to my father's collection of LP records, and a Czech Philharmonic recording of Bedřich Smetana's Má vlast ("My Fatherland"), a series of six symphonic tone poems celebrating Czech countryside, history and legend, the best-known being Vltava ("The Moldau"). Written in the late 19th century, this work was embraced by Czechs as an unofficial national anthem, and continues to be widely popular. My father must have enjoyed this music, and likely purchased the LP on one of his trips to Czechoslovakia.

Album cover of the Supraphon recording of Má vlast that first introduced me to this music. (*Supraphon*)

The class assignment required me to listen closely to the music, and I came to deeply appreciate it. From then on, Má vlast provided me with an emotional connection to my Czech roots, and also to my father. This connection deepened following his death, and has become a cherished piece of music that often brings up tears.

10

Final Years

The last few years of my father's life were perhaps the best and most settled in his adult life. The Weiss Travel Bureau continued to be a viable business as it navigated the changing landscape of the travel industry. While this required nimble adjustments in the face of growing competition from the charter companies, and the shifting complexities of international regulations and country-specific rules, the expanding market of destinations and air routes encouraged Americans to explore the world.

It was during these years that Jack witnessed his sons growing into adulthood and graduating from college. Both he and Joy placed great importance on education for their children, and made it possible for us to pursue whatever path this might take. We both chose small prestigious liberal arts colleges on the east coast, Eric to Wesleyan University (in Middletown, CT) and me to Haverford College (in suburban Philadelphia). Our parents likely enjoyed life as empty nesters, but they visited us on a few occasions, including our college graduations.

Family photo at my college graduation. (May 1976)

Jack continued his world travels in the early 1970s, visiting Yugoslavia, Israel, California, Hawaii, South America and the Caribbean. Mostly, these were vacations with Joy, and some included cruises. It was during this period that Jack twice returned to his country of birth, in 1973 and again in 1975. Czechoslovakia remained firmly behind the Iron Curtain, but these trips were mostly for personal reasons to visit cousins in Prague and his childhood places in Plzeň (where photos show he visited his mother's gravesite) and his grandfather's farm in Lasovice.

Jack posing at his childhood homes. (December 1975)

It was on the last trip that Jack had an unexpected encounter while revisiting his childhood summer memories in Lasovice. As he strolled around the village, an old woman suddenly emerged from a house and announced to my father that she knew him, and had been waiting for his return. As it turned out, before Jack's family was rounded up by the Germans in 1942, she was entrusted to hold onto some of their family photos and other possessions. Now, more than 30 years later, she was finally able to hand them back.[57]

Unlike my mother, my father never seemed to put much attention into personal introspection and psychological self-improvement. This began to change in the early 1970s as Jack entered his 50s, and his life became more settled with children out of the house and his business on firm ground. Joy was especially keen on her current therapist, and convinced Jack that he too should begin the important "work" of addressing his unresolved internal conflicts. Exactly how he proceeded and what impact this had on him goes unrecorded. But the one tangible result was the 11-page autobiographical statement he was assigned to write in May 1973, many parts of which are excerpted in these pages.

It was in this statement that Jack opened up about how he felt in that moment about his life. He wrote about his work ("I have always loved my work and still do"), his concerns about the future for his sons, and the continued challenges posed by his marriage ("Joy is the only one and the only thing in my life I have never solved and it must be that which is getting me down"). He summed it all up as follows:

> I had always thought that I sailed a pretty good course, not an even one or a straight one as the damned wind keeps knocking me down. But I have never stayed down for long, and certainly never as long as now. Perhaps it's time [to] change course again and try a completely different tack and if you can help me do that I shall be forever grateful.

What did he mean by "staying down for long and certainly never as long as now"? I was never privy to my father's internal feelings, and perhaps he was suffering from depression and had been for some time. Being away at college in these years, I simply didn't see enough of him to appreciate what he may have been going through. And, of course, there must have been trauma associated with the loss of his family in the Holocaust, which never appeared on the surface but must have been at play.

My father flashes his wonderful smile. (December 1975)

I graduated from college in May 1976, and had the summer to look forward to before returning to Philadelphia to look for work while taking the year to decide about graduate school. It was the summer to fulfill my longtime dream of seeing California as part of a cross-country road trip adventure. The night before I left, I gave my father a copy of my newly-minted resume, in part to show off what I'd accomplished and also just in case he could pass it on to some potential employer while I was away. I recall him looking at my resume and telling me that he would never consider hiring me because I was clearly so overqualified. Why should I remember this moment so clearly? Perhaps I was initially confused by his joke, or maybe I simply appreciated the compliment behind it. It was the last time I would see him.

My travels took me through the American southwest and was later joined by my college friend Joey Grodman, with whom I finally arrived in southern California. After spending a week or so enjoying the ocean, visiting Disneyland and the Hollywood Bowl, we drove inland to the Sierra Nevada mountains to spend a few days camping and hiking in the fabled Yosemite National Park. The evening before we left, I called home as I did every few weeks to check in and let my parents know I was OK. It was an uneventful call, but would be the last time I would hear my father's voice.

The next day, Joey and I took a final morning hike, then drove back out of the mountains to the coast. We arrived at Morro Bay State Park late that afternoon. After finding a campsite, I used a payphone to call my housemates back in Philadelphia to connect with my friend Mike Raciti, who was to meet up with us shortly in San Francisco.

Whoever answered the phone in Philadelphia told me to call home right away. When my mother answered, I somehow knew what she would say the moment before she spoke. My father had died earlier that day. The previous day he was at work at his desk when he suddenly collapsed from a cerebral hemorrhage. Jack was rushed to a hospital and survived the night, but would not last another day. My mother made desperate efforts to contact me. She contacted Yosemite and was told we had checked out. With the help of family friends, she notified the California Highway Patrol to put out an all-points bulletin for my car; it was lemon yellow and should have been easy to spot. By the time I finally called home, he was gone.

Morro Bay, California. (*Morro Bay Rock, Clinton Steeds*)

That moment remains with me to this day. Standing in that lone phone booth with a 360-degree vista of the Pacific Ocean and coastal hills. I was completely stunned and in shock. I found my way back to the campsite and struggled to make sense of what had just happened. I was incredibly fortunate to be travelling with Joey, who happened to be just the right kind of person one needs in this situation. He knew how to look after me that very difficult night, and got me on an early morning flight out of Santa Barbara that would take me back to Chicago.[58]

Once back home, I remember very little of what transpired over the subsequent period. There was a memorial service for my father, and I recall being there. There seemed to be a lot of people in attendance, his therapist was one of the speakers, they played Smetana's Vltava, and I did a lot of crying. I don't believe his body was present at the service, so he may have been cremated by then. Sometime that fall my mother spread his ashes in Lake Michigan from our family friend's sailboat.

o o o o

My grieving period was short, and the loss receded quickly into the background as I moved into my early adult years. I would think of my father from time to time, and this would prompt a heartfelt feeling that was both sad and sweet; it was a good feeling.

Growing up, I never felt like I needed my father (apart from the material support he so generously provided), likely because he wasn't often present and our relationship was conflicted. But once he was gone, I began to identify with him as I never did while he was alive, and to find a personal strength in this. I felt inspired by what I knew of his life story, in escaping the Holocaust and creating a new life for himself at such a young age. I felt proud of his role in WWII and his career as a world travelling "jet setter." And I came to recognize and value his personal qualities of generosity and attention to other people; his adeptness in navigating challenging situations; his respect for and treatment of women; and what to me seemed like confidence and comfort in his own skin. And this helped me better understand and appreciate the extent to which I see some of these same qualities in myself.

So, in the end, I've found a great relationship with my father even if this lives in my head and we can't enjoy it together. Of course, I dearly miss so many years of my life without him, and the opportunity of getting to know each other as adults. I'm sure we would have grown closer and enjoyed each other in ways I can only dream about.

I also very much regret that Jack never got to meet my own family: my wife, children and grandchildren. I have absolutely no doubt he would have loved them all unreservedly, and they would have equally loved him back. He would have made such an awesome grandfather.

And, finally, I regret not being there for his last hours or minutes of life, to have a chance to see him one last time, to say goodbye and tell him what else was in my heart with that last opportunity to do so.

It was such a tragic loss to lose my father so soon. And yet, I've also come to find meaning and perhaps purpose in these circumstances. I think about our difficulties as father and son, and losing him before we truly found each other as adults. This experience has been formative for me in who

I have become; just as Jack's early and sudden separation from his own father at an even younger age shaped his life as it unfolded.

We may wish for a life that follows a smooth unbroken path, but sometimes there is purpose when it challenges us in uncomfortable ways. This idea is powerfully articulated by the Jewish rabbi and writer Alan Lew when he contemplated his own childhood:

> My soul needed that struggle. It had needed to do this so that it could struggle up to the surface of the world and form itself in this struggle... It was, in fact, my parents' job to provide me with this impediment, to give my soul something... to express itself by overcoming.[59]

How would Jack look back on his life story were he alive today? The 11-page statement he wrote a few years before his death offers an invaluable glimpse, but also reflects his perspective at a particular time when he was feeling low and seeking help. What he also left behind was a rich trove of documents and photos in which a more complete picture of the man could be found. Whether or not he intended anyone to dig into this material and uncover the story, it was truly a wonderful gift to leave those of us who knew and loved him.

Jack with his boys in Spain. (1961)

Acknowledgements

My first debt of gratitude is to members of my family, who provided material for this story that added to my own recollections and research: my brother Eric Neuman; my father's first cousin Gianni Neumann (his sole surviving Czech contemporary); and my American cousins: Susie Boyer, Noel Davis, Beth Fisher, Lester Fisher, Jane Hannuksela, Herb Lederer, Robert Lederer, Kate Mayberry, Margot Molay, Jessie Walker, Marjorie Walker and Ellen Wolff. They proved to be a keen audience as the chapters rolled out one-by-one, and offered enthusiastic encouragement to keep going. Each of them knew Jack Neuman in his lifetime, but (as with me) none ever knew his full story until now.

I also owe thanks to those who provided key information about the history of the Ritchie Boys, including essential details about my father's service record: Dr. David S. Frey (Director, Center for Holocaust and Genocide Studies, U.S. Military Academy), Stephen Goodale, Dan Gross, Bruce Henderson, and Bernard Lubran.

The publication of this work was ably supported by the effective copyediting by Cathy McKim, the elegant typesetting by Nick May from TypeRight, and the helpful advice about self-publishing by brother-in-law Jamie Campbell. The cover design was created by my talented son Alex Neuman.

Finally, I am grateful for the everlasting support and encouragement from my wife Joan Campbell, who also contributed her professional skills in the preparation of the photos appearing in this book. She never got the chance to meet my father, but I'm sure they would have become fast friends.

Sources

As this is a personal memoir, the primary source material is the great number of personal documents and photos belonging to (and inexplicably kept by) my father, encompassing almost the entirety of his life. Also important to the story is my mother's partly completed autobiography, and personal recollections provided to me by my brother Eric, and by extended family members still living who knew and loved Jack Neuman.

Other source material is referenced in endnotes and in photo credits where applicable.

Endnotes

1   Helen Epstein, *Where She Came From: A Daughter's Search for her Mother's History* (Little Brown & Company, 1997), p. 50

2   Ibid., p.142

3   My father wrote that his was the only Jewish family in the village, but recently I was contacted by a distant cousin whose Jewish grandmother also lived there, and who sent postcards of travels to Jack's father when they were both in their teens.

4   I should point out that, as his son, I never ever noticed anything unusual about my father's face, and even when I study photos, I have difficulty seeing how one side looks different from the other. My brother Eric, however, recalls being aware of the scars.

5   The new U.S. immigration policy was instituted in 1930 by President Herbert Hoover to stem the flow of immigrants during the Depression. The new policy required that an affidavit be signed by a U.S. guardian guaranteeing the immigrant in question would not end up on the public dole.

6   The document referenced is a "legalized translation" of the original Czech version. The translation into English was done (or perhaps required) so that it would be readable to officials upon landing in the U.S. This version was produced by an interpreter (Rose Nemetz-ova) "nominated by the decree of the Supreme Court of Prague," who certified by oath "that it was in complete accordance with the original written in Czech."

7   The MV Saturnia was an Italian ocean liner that served the route between Italy and New York for several decades before WWII. The voyage transporting my father proved to be its last in this transatlantic capacity, and near the end of the war was converted into an American hospital ship. Today, there is a life ring from the Saturnia affixed to an exterior wall in the historic Italian neighbourhood of my home city of Ottawa Canada, as part of a heritage mural commemorating the city's Italian community (pictured elsewhere in this book).

8   Josef Neumann was the only one of my father's uncles and aunts to survive the war. He and his family were interned in a small village in Southern Italy. His son Hanus (now Gianni) reconnected with my father after the war, and now lives in Piacenza Italy. He has become a close friend, and my one surviving Neumann relative from that generation.

9   There is in fact documentation that a French submarine stopped the Saturnia in mid-ocean on December 16, 1939, and removed "seven Jewish passengers of German origin. This is referenced in a history of the ship on the website Italian Ocean Liners. https://www.italianliners.com/

10   Franz Seidler is mentioned briefly in a letter my father received from his father around that time, as someone in NYC who my father should contact. The only other information of note comes from my cousin Gianni Neumann (one of Jack's two first cousins and who survived the war). Gianni recalls staying briefly with a Pepi Seidler in NYC in 1956.

11   The personalized autograph (in green ink) is certainly authentic, although there is no actual reference to The Cotton Club on the photograph (it credits a NYC photographer). Louis Armstrong definitely played this venue, which closed permanently later in 1940.

12   This story comes from my brother Eric, who remembers hearing it from our dad.

13   Isenberg and Sons started as a dressmaker, but moved into jewelry, for which it gained a reputation as making the best quality costume jewelry (often referred to as "Isenberg Ice" – still a hot item among collectors).

14 This description of Camp Barkeley comes from the memoir of a fellow soldier, as recounted in Bruce Henderson's book *Sons and Soldiers* (pp. 154-155).

15 In 1942 the British military established a secret corps of commandos composed mostly of Jewish refugees, as described in Leah Barrett's book *X Troop: The Secret Jewish Commandos of World War II* (Houghton Mifflin Harcourt, 2021).

16 Bruce Henderson, *Sons and Soldiers* (William Morrow, 2014). pp. 132-133.

17 Ibid., p.157.

18 https://www.imdb.com/title/tt0435725/

19 First aired May 9, 2021.

20 I am indebted to Stephen Goodell, who provided me with the names of IPW 879. Rudy Michaelis was one of the Ritchie Boys featured in the Christian Bauer documentary, so listening to his stories in the field gives me a sense of my father's stories as well. This may have been his initial team, but in an MIS order dated October 18, 1944, he is listed as part of another team (MII Team 440G), also attached to the 5th Armored Division.

21 "Dog tags" were identification tags worn by U.S. Army personnel, which took the form of small rectangular metal plates stamped with the name, ID number, blood type and religion (e.g., "J" for Jewish). They typically came in pairs and attached to a light metal chain. Jack kept his dog tags, and they are now part of the collection of his wartime memorabilia.

22 My brother Eric also recalls hearing this story, and believes it likely to be true.

23 *Sons and Soldiers*, p.258.

24 This incident was described in detail in Bruce Henderson's book. The two Team members were T/5 Murray Zappler and S/Sgt Kurt Jacobs with the IPW Team 154, both of whom were originally from Berlin. The German officer, Captain Curt Bruns was subsequently captured, tried and convicted of these murders; he himself was executed by firing squad in June 1945.

25   SHAEF was the headquarters of the Commander of Allied forces in Northwest Europe from late 1943 until the end of World War II, under the command of the Supreme Commander, U.S. General Dwight D. Eisenhower.

26   Rose was Louis Fisher's eldest daughter, and formed a close bond with Jack when he arrived in Chicago. It was Rose who secured Jack's offer of enrollment at the YMCA College that made his student visa possible. In 2000, she sent me the letters, which she found in her attic and felt I should have. She was one of my favourite Czech cousins during my childhood years.

27   I obtained a copy of the records with these dates from a Jewish memorial centre in Plzeň on a visit in 2003.

28   Otto Oplatka apparently took a lead role in pulling together the all-important affidavit signed by Rose's father, Louis Fisher.

29   Andrey Vlasov was a Soviet Red Army general and Nazi collaborator. During World War II, he fought in the Battle of Moscow and was later captured attempting to lift the siege of Leningrad. After being captured, he defected to Nazi Germany and headed the Russian Liberation Army to aid the Nazis in liberating Russia from the Soviets. At the war's end, he changed sides once again and sided with the Czech resistance fighters in the Prague uprising against the Germans.

30   My brother Eric recalls a conversation with our father in which he said that "breaking" the men he interrogated led him to later sympathize with them as humans like him, not the monsters they were made out to be.

31   The documentation consists of a faded deposit slip, and certified translation issued by a Chicago-based Notary Public.

32   Also on the same reassignment order was Tech 3 Kurt Rosenow, another Ritchie Boy, who upon release from active duty would become the first Director of the Berlin Document Center in 1946.

33   Mary Williams Walsh, *LA Times*, 1994. As documented by Dan Gross (personal correspondence).

34 Erika Mann, *Philadelphia Inquirer*, March 3, 1946.

35 Gerald Posner, Letter from Berlin, *The New Yorker*, March 14, 1994.

36 From Herbert Murez, a Ritchie Boy assigned to the BDC, via personal correspondence.

37 The GI Bill was passed by Congress in 1944 to provide a range of benefits to returning war veterans. Benefits included low-cost mortgages; low-interest loans to start a business or farm; one year of unemployment benefits; and payments of tuition and living expenses to attend high school, college or vocational school. As of 1956, 7.8 million veterans made use of the education benefits.

38 He also received a job offer from American Express, but the pay was lower and it might have required relocation anywhere in the country. This was out of the question for Joy, who was employed with a job she loved. Jack might have been hesitant to move yet again to another unknown part of the country and far away from his cousins.

39 The Czech communists closed the border on February 28, 1948.

40 These documents were likely translated into English for the benefit of Jack's American and English lawyers.

41 This amount would be roughly equivalent to $38,000 USD in 1939.

42 This hearkens back to the financial problem Adolf raised a couple of years later in one of his letters to his son in America.

43 This earlier date was used because the appraiser did not consider the current market to be applicable as "the building serves mainly business purposes and with reference to the law of protection of tenants and the unstable rental conditions in Plzeň" at that time.

44 Demela, J.& S. Mikula, Private property in Communist Czechoslovakia. *Review of Economic Perspectives*, Volume 15, 3, 2015.

45   The amounts paid out were apportioned in specified shares to myself, my brother Eric and my cousin Gianni. One-half of Max Immergut's policy was apportioned to his family heirs, but I never learned if any were still living.

46   This was not an inexpensive experience. In these early years, a roundtrip transatlantic flight to Europe could cost the equivalent of $3,000 in today's dollars.

47   These details are listed in an Army Reserve Corps questionnaire he completed in April 1949.

48   Up until the mid-1990s, all airline tickets were in paper form with carbon copies, printed by airlines and travel agents.

49   The series came about through my parents' long-time friendship with Murray and Judy Flander, who published the *Victor Press* at the time.

50   My father's younger cousin Petr Marek (who lived in Prague) travelled to the U.S. sometime in the 1960s. He seriously considered staying, but in the end returned home to his aging parents.

51   We visited the Rosebud Reservation to check out an exchange program, in which a non-Indian youth spent a summer on the reservation with an Indian family, and the next year a youth from the Indian family spent the summer with the non-Indian family. My parents thought this sounded like a great idea, but as a nine-year-old I wasn't prepared for the poverty on the reservation and backed out of the program.

52   The first organized tours to the Galapagos Islands began in 1969.

53   My mother writes that Dr. Mead considered her to be her "star patient," given her dramatic turnaround in the matter of wanting children.

54   What I remember from that game is asking him which team he was rooting for, and being greatly surprised when he said the U.S. team. I couldn't understand why he wouldn't support the team from his native country. But at that point, of course, I had not read his newspaper series about life under Communist rule.

55 Neither Eric nor I have any recollection of these brunch parties, and wonder if this is because we were shipped off to our grandparents at these times. It is my cousin Gianni Neumann who clearly remembers these parties when he briefly stayed at our house for a month or two in 1957.

56 Jack found a way to import his favourite beer by the case in the early 1970s, long before it was available commercially in liquor stores. He justified it by telling us that his doctor told him that drinking one beer every day would help prevent kidney stones (which he once suffered through). He reasoned that beer from his home town would be especially therapeutic.

57 I don't recall ever hearing this story from my father. It comes from one of his contemporaries, my cousin Beth Fisher (Les Fisher's first wife), who heard about it from Jack when he returned from the trip, and remembered it clearly when I interviewed her early in 2021. There is no doubt that what changed hands in Lasovice that day ended up in mine as I assembled material for this story.

58 Joey's counselling skills would lead him to establish a successful psychotherapy practice in Chicago.

59 Alan Lew, *This is real and you are completely unprepared* (Little Brown and Company, 2003)

About the Author

Keith Neuman's professional career has been devoted to conducting social research to help society understand itself better, and over the past four decades has written several hundred research reports. This is his first book. Keith lives with his wife in Ottawa, Ontario.